MILITARY AND VETERAN ISSUES

SEXUAL ASSAULTS OF MALE MILITARY PERSONNEL

MILITARY AND VETERAN ISSUES

Additional books in this series can be found on Nova's website under the Series tab.

Additional e-books in this series can be found on Nova's website under the e-book tab.

MILITARY AND VETERAN ISSUES

SEXUAL ASSAULTS OF MALE MILITARY PERSONNEL

HENRIETTA MOORE
EDITOR

NOVINKA
New York

NOTICE TO THE READER

Library of Congress Cataloging-in-Publication Data

ISBN: 978-1-63483-564-0

Published by Nova Science Publishers, Inc. † New York

CONTENTS

PREFACE

Females have long been viewed as the primary victims of sexual assault but, based on survey data, RAND estimated that in 2014, about 9,000 to about 13,000 male servicemembers were sexually assaulted. This book addresses the extent to which DOD has taken actions to prevent and respond to sexual assaults of male servicemembers; DOD's sexual assault prevention and response program is meeting the medical and mental health-care needs of male servicemembers; and the culture of the U.S. military poses distinct challenges for preventing and responding to sexual assaults of male servicemembers.

In: Sexual Assaults of Male Military Personnel ISBN: 978-1-63483-564-0
Editor: Henrietta Moore

Chapter 1

MILITARY PERSONNEL: ACTIONS NEEDED TO ADDRESS SEXUAL ASSAULTS OF MALE SERVICEMEMBERS*

United States Government Accountability Office

WHY GAO DID THIS STUDY

Females have long been viewed as the primary victims of sexual assault but, based on survey data, RAND estimated that in 2014, about 9,000 to about 13,000 male servicemembers were sexually assaulted. The House report accompanying the Fiscal Year 2014 National Defense Authorization Act mandated that GAO review DOD's efforts to address sexual assaults of male servicemembers.

This report addresses the extent to which (1) DOD has taken actions to prevent and respond to sexual assaults of male servicemembers, (2) DOD's sexual assault prevention and response program is meeting the medical and mental health-care needs of male servicemembers, and (3) the culture of the U.S. military poses distinct challenges for preventing and responding to sexual assaults of male servicemembers. GAO reviewed DOD reports and strategies; analyzed data on sexual assaults from surveys and reported incidents from

---

* This is an edited, reformatted and augmented version of a United States Government Accountability Office publication, No. GAO-15-284, dated March 2015.

fiscal years 2008 through 2014; and interviewed DOD officials with related program responsibilities.

WHAT GAO RECOMMENDS

GAO recommends, among other things, that DOD develop a plan for using its data to inform program development; systematically evaluate whether male victims have gender-specific medical and mental healthcare needs; develop goals and metrics; and revise training to address male victims. DOD concurred with all recommendations.

WHAT GAO FOUND

The Department of Defense (DOD) has taken steps to address sexual assaults of servicemembers generally, but it has not used all of its data, such as analyses that show significantly fewer male servicemembers than females reporting when they are sexually assaulted, to inform program decision making. In 2014, DOD data show that 1,180 males and 4,104 females reported a sexual assault to DOD. GAO's analysis of sexual assault prevalence estimates using the results of a study conducted for DOD by the RAND Corporation shows that at most 13 percent of males reported their assaults, whereas at least 40 percent of females reported. DOD has recently begun to develop ideas for increasing male reporting, such as further outreach. DOD has reported data on the gender of military sexual assault victims since 2008, but it has not used all these data to inform program decision making or established a plan to do so. Since 2008, GAO has reported on limitations in DOD's use of data to inform decision making in its sexual assault prevention and response program, and recommended that DOD take action in response, but problems persist. Thus, without a plan for how it will use data in making decisions about program development, DOD risks leaving important issues, such as those related to male victims, unaddressed.

DOD has taken steps to provide and improve the availability of medical and mental health care for all sexual assault victims, but DOD's Health Affairs office has not systematically identified whether male victims have any gender-specific needs. DOD sexual assault policies specify that care be sensitive to gender-specific issues. Care providers and experts said that male victims may have different responses to the trauma than females, such as questioning their masculinity and their sexuality. In 2008, DOD recognized that more information was needed on the needs of males who are sexually assaulted but did not identify those needs. DOD stated in its April 2014 prevention strategy that it intends to research the situations leading to male victimization and the needs of male victims, and has begun to collect information toward this objective with its 2014 Military Workplace Study. However, until DOD's Health Affairs office systematically evaluates the medical and mental health-care needs of male victims, it will be difficult for DOD to help its providers maximize the effectiveness of the care that they provide to male sexual assault victims.

DOD has recognized that a cultural change is needed to address sexual assaults, but has not yet taken several key steps to further this change. In reports and interviews, DOD has identified that military culture can pose challenges to effectively implementing a program to prevent sexual assault. For example, in 2008, DOD acknowledged that it would need to address the "unofficial" culture that is defined by exaggerated characteristics of stereotypical masculinity, among other things, and is linked to values and customs that perpetuate rape. Key practices for implementing organizational transformations, such as cultural changes, include establishing and measuring progress toward performance goals and training employees as a means to effect the desired change. DOD has not established goals or metrics to gauge sexual assault–related issues for male servicemembers, and has also generally not portrayed male sexual assault victims in its sexual assault prevention training material. Actions to address these issues could help DOD effect the change it states is needed to effectively prevent and respond to sexual assaults of male servicemembers.

ABBREVIATIONS

DOD	Department of Defense
SAPRO	Sexual Assault Prevention and Response Office
UCMJ	Uniform Code of Military Justice
VA	Department of Veterans Affairs
WGRA	Workplace and Gender Relations Survey of Active Duty Members

March 19, 2015
The Honorable Mac Thornberry
Chairman

The Honorable Adam Smith
Ranking Member

Committee on Armed Services
House of Representatives

Culturally, females have long been viewed as the primary victims in sexual assault–related crimes. For example, up until January 1, 2013, the Uniform Crime Reports—an annual publication in which the Federal Bureau of Investigation compiles data on crimes that occur nationwide and within the Department of Defense (DOD)—defined rape as, "the carnal knowledge of a female forcibly and against her will."[1] However, sexual assaults of males—both within and outside of the U.S. military— are not a new phenomenon. For fiscal years 2008 through 2014, DOD data show that at least 3,200 male servicemembers reported being sexually assaulted.[2] Further, sexual assault is a generally underreported crime, and based on a survey of active-duty servicemembers conducted by the RAND Corporation in 2014, it is estimated that about 9,000 to 13,000 male active-duty servicemembers were sexually assaulted in the year prior to the survey, of which about 2,500 to 5,500 were penetrative sexual assaults.[3]

For more than a decade, Congress and DOD have taken a variety of steps intended to generally prevent and respond to sexual assault in the military. In 2004, following a series of high-profile sexual assault cases involving servicemembers, Congress required the Secretary of Defense to develop, among other things, a comprehensive policy for DOD on the prevention of and response to sexual assaults involving servicemembers.[4] In response to statutory requirements, DOD established its sexual assault prevention and response program in 2005 to promote prevention, encourage increased reporting of sexual assault-crimes, and improve victim response capabilities. Since 2005, there have been numerous statutory provisions aimed at improving the department's program to prevent, respond to, and resolve sexual assault incidents, including mandating that the program's Director position be filled by at least a general or flag officer or comparable civilian employee from the Senior Executive Service.

From 2008 through 2014, we issued multiple reports that reviewed various aspects of DOD's sexual assault prevention and response program. For example, in August 2008, we found, among other things, that (1) DOD's guidance did not adequately address some important issues, such as how to implement the sexual assault prevention and response program when operating in a deployed environment or in joint environments; (2) not all commanders supported the department's sexual assault prevention and response programs, though most did; (3) required sexual assault prevention and response training was not consistently effective; and (4) factors such as a DOD-reported shortage of mental health-care providers affected whether servicemembers who are victims of sexual assault can or do access mental health services. We made nine recommendations to the Secretary of Defense to improve the oversight and implementation of DOD's program, such as to develop an oversight framework that contains long-term goals, objectives, and milestones in addition to performance goals, strategies to be used to accomplish goals, and criteria for measuring progress; assess commanders' support of the sexual assault prevention program; review and revise guidance and training; review victims' access to mental health care; and evaluate appropriate staffing levels of certain sexual assault response–related positions.[5]

Additionally, in February 2010, we reviewed DOD's progress in addressing our August 2008 recommendations and found that the department's draft oversight framework lacked key elements needed for comprehensive oversight of DOD's programs, such as criteria for measuring progress and an indication of how DOD would use the information derived from such measurement to improve its programs. We made recommendations to help ensure that DOD was assessing the development of future programs to improve its overall response to sexual assault.[6] DOD concurred or partially concurred with recommendations from our 2008 and 2010 reports and has since taken actions to address all of these recommendations. Also, in January 2013, we reported on the extent to which medical and mental health care were available to servicewomen who were victims of sexual assault.[7] We found that several factors, such as branch of military service and operational uncertainties of a deployed environment, affected the extent to which such care was available. We recommended that DOD develop and implement guidance on the provision of care that specifies providers' responsibilities to respond to and care for sexual assault victims, whether in the United States or in deployed environments. We also recommended that DOD take steps to improve compliance regarding the completion of annual refresher training on sexual assault prevention and response. DOD did not concur with the first recommendation[8] and concurred with the second recommendation. However, DOD subsequently included guidance on healthcare provider responsibilities in its instruction on the sexual assault prevention and response program. In addition, DOD subsequently directed annual training requirements and standards for sexual assault first responders, and required the services to report progress in monitoring sexual assault training. For a list of related reports, see the Related GAO Products page at the end of this report.

In June 2013, the House Armed Services Committee raised the issue of whether DOD has focused on efforts to assist male servicemembers. 9 The House Report accompanying the National Defense Authorization Act for Fiscal Year 2014 mandated that we review the extent to which the culture of the military poses unique challenges for preventing and responding to sexual assaults of male servicemembers, what steps DOD has taken to address the incidence of and response to male servicemembers who are sexually assaulted, and whether DOD has established policies and protocols for the provision of medical and mental health care to address sexual trauma given the unique requirements for male victims of sexual assault.[10] This report addresses the extent to which (1) DOD has taken actions to prevent and respond to sexual assaults of male servicemembers, (2) DOD's sexual assault prevention and response program is meeting the medical and mental health-care needs of male victims of sexual assault, and (3) the culture of the U.S. military poses distinct challenges for preventing and responding to sexual assaults of male servicemembers.

To evaluate the extent to which DOD has taken steps to prevent and respond to sexual assaults of male servicemembers, we reviewed DOD's and the military services' relevant guidance and requirements, including reports and strategies on preventing and responding to sexual assault, and analyzed DOD data on servicemembers who reported a sexual assault incident in fiscal years 2008 through 2014.[11] We also reviewed DOD and RAND Corporation estimates[12] of servicemembers subjected to unwanted sexual contact or sexually assaulted in fiscal years 2010, 2012, and 2014.[13] We assessed the reliability of DOD's data on the number of reported victims of sexual assault by gender by (1) performing electronic testing for obvious errors in accuracy and completeness, (2) reviewing existing information about the data and the systems that produced them, and (3) interviewing agency officials knowledgeable about the data. In reviewing documentation from DOD's Workplace and Gender Relations Survey of Active Duty Members for fiscal years 2010 and 2012, we found the survey results of the estimated prevalence of unwanted sexual contact by gender to be sufficiently reliable for the purposes we use them in this report. In reviewing DOD's Report to the President of the United States on Sexual Assault Prevention and Response that includes data from the 2014 Military Workplace Study from the RAND Corporation, we found the survey results of the estimated prevalence of unwanted sexual contact and sexual assault by gender to be sufficiently reliable for the purposes of our report. To assess the reliability of these data, we reviewed survey documentation and interviewed officials in DOD's Sexual Assault Prevention and Response Office (SAPRO) and those from the RAND Corporation who are knowledgeable about these data. We also interviewed various officials with responsibilities related to the prevention of and response to sexual assaults and randomly selected male servicemembers at four military installations—one per service—in the United States to obtain their perspectives on DOD's efforts to prevent and respond to sexual assaults of male servicemembers.[14] At our installation visits, we met with sexual assault response coordinators; victim advocates; special victims' counsel; chaplains; medical and mental health personnel; and commanders. We also obtained male servicemembers' perspectives through an interviewer-administered survey of 122 randomly selected male servicemembers within four rank categories from across the four military installations.[15] In addition, we interviewed current and former male servicemembers who were victims of sexual assault and volunteered to speak with us about their perspectives on the military and its response to sexual assaults.[16] We also compared DOD's rationale for how it prioritizes its sexual assault prevention and response efforts with leading practices for results-oriented management to determine the extent to which DOD uses the data it collects on sexual assault incidents to focus its program efforts.[17]

To evaluate the extent to which DOD's sexual assault prevention and response program is meeting the medical and mental health-care needs of male victims of sexual assault, we reviewed DOD's and the military services' relevant guidance and requirements; interviewed health-care and program officials at the four military installations we visited; and asked male victims for their perspectives on the military's response to and health-care services offered following their sexual assault. We conducted a literature review of academic and research articles published from January 2008 through September 2014 that addressed the incidence of and how male victims may respond to sexual assaults in order to identify any findings and research on differences in how males and females respond to sexual assault as well as gender-specific needs of male victims. We also compared DOD's current guidance on providing gender-responsive care to sexual assault victims with leading practices for program evaluation to determine the extent to which DOD has systematically evaluated program needs.[18] We interviewed subject-matter experts, healthcare providers, and advocacy groups that were selected based on their experience working with male victims of sexual assault. While the views of subject-matter experts, health-care providers, and advocacy groups are not generalizable across any population, they enabled us to obtain the views of non-DOD experts who have experience working with male victims of sexual assault.

To evaluate the extent to which the culture of the U.S. military poses distinct challenges for preventing and responding to sexual assaults of male servicemembers, we reviewed DOD's and the military services' relevant guidance and requirements; interviewed installation officials as described above and conducted an interviewer-administered nongeneralizable survey of randomly selected male servicemembers of various ranks to gain their perspectives on barriers to reporting a sexual assault; and used our interviews with male victims for additional information on whether military culture plays a role in the incidence of and response to sexual assault. For each of the four installations we visited, we obtained and reviewed reports containing the results of surveys administered by unit commanders in order to: (1) review servicemember comments related to the environment at their command; (2) identify what sexual assault prevention and response–related questions they contained; and (3) review the recommendations for commanders included in the reports. We obtained sexual assault training materials from each military service and reviewed the extent to which they address the sexual victimization of males, discuss activities such as hazing that may constitute a sexual assault, and include slides directly applicable to leadership and command-climate issues. We reviewed relevant reports and studies on the subject of sexual assault in the military and discussed the topic with the subject-matter experts noted above. We also compared steps DOD has taken on sexual assault prevention and response with leading practices for organizational change to determine what, if any, steps DOD could take to foster an environment in which male servicemembers are more likely to report that they have been sexually assaulted.[19] Additional information about our scope and methodology can be found in appendix I.

We conducted this performance audit from November 2013 to March 2015 in accordance with generally accepted government auditing standards. Those standards require that we plan and perform the audit to obtain sufficient, appropriate evidence to provide a reasonable basis for our findings and conclusions based on our audit objectives. We believe that the evidence obtained provides a reasonable basis for our findings and conclusions based on our audit objectives.

BACKGROUND

Sexual Assault Definition

DOD formally defines sexual assault as intentional sexual contact, characterized by use of force, threats, intimidation, abuse of authority, or when the victim does not or cannot consent. The term includes a broad category of sexual offenses consisting of the following specific Uniform Code of Military Justice (UCMJ) offenses: rape, sexual assault, aggravated sexual contact, abusive sexual contact, forcible sodomy (forced oral or anal sex), or attempts to commit these acts.[20]

DOD's Sexual Assault Prevention and Response Program

Since establishing the sexual assault prevention and response program in 2005, DOD has undertaken a variety of initiatives both to prevent sexual assaults from occurring and to increase the department's visibility over and awareness of sexual assault incidents that do occur. For example, DOD and each of the military services developed and implemented strategies aimed at preventing sexual assault incidents from occurring. DOD also implemented a number of strategies aimed at increasing the number of victims willing to report that they were sexually assaulted and at improving response capabilities to sexual assaults. Specifically, since 2005, in response to statutory requirements, DOD has provided active-duty servicemembers with two options for reporting a sexual assault: (1) restricted and (2) unrestricted. DOD's restricted reporting option allows sexual assault victims to confidentially disclose an alleged sexual assault to select individuals and receive medical and mental healthcare treatment without initiating an official investigation. In cases where a victim elects restricted reporting, first responders may not disclose confidential communications to law-enforcement or command authorities unless certain exceptions apply, and improper disclosure of confidential communications and medical information may result in discipline pursuant to the UCMJ or other adverse personnel actions. In contrast, DOD's unrestricted reporting option also triggers an investigation by a military criminal investigative organization. In an effort to increase victims' confidence in the military justice process and to encourage reporting, DOD revised its sexual assault prevention and response policy in January 2012 to protect victims of sexual assault from coercion, retaliation, and reprisal.[21] In an April 2012 memorandum, the Secretary of Defense withheld, in certain sexual assault cases, the disposition authority under the UCMJ from commanders who are not a special court-martial convening authority and in the grade of O-6 or higher (that is, at least a Colonel in the Army, Marine Corps, or Air Force, or a Captain in the Navy).[22]

Various offices and organizations in DOD play a role in preventing and responding to sexual assault within the military. The Under Secretary of Defense for Personnel and Readiness is responsible for developing the overall policy and guidance for the department's sexual assault prevention and response program except for criminal investigative policy matters assigned to the DOD Inspector General and legal processes in the UCMJ. Accordingly, the Under Secretary of Defense for Personnel and Readiness oversees SAPRO, which serves as the department's single point of authority, accountability, and oversight for its sexual assault prevention and response program. The responsibilities of the Under Secretary of Defense for Personnel and Readiness and SAPRO with regard to sexual assault prevention and response include providing the military services with guidance and technical support and facilitating the identification and resolution of issues; developing programs, policies, and training standards for the prevention of, reporting of, and response to sexual assault, including the provision of health care for sexual assault victims; developing strategic program guidance and joint planning objectives; overseeing the department's collection and maintenance of data on reported alleged sexual assaults involving servicemembers; establishing mechanisms to measure the effectiveness of the department's sexual assault prevention and response program; and preparing the department's mandated annual reports to Congress on sexual assaults involving servicemembers.[23]

In addition, the Assistant Secretary of Defense for Health Affairs is responsible for advising the Under Secretary of Defense for Personnel and Readiness on DOD's sexual assault health-care policies, clinical-practice guidelines, related procedures and standards of the DOD healthcare programs for sexual assault victims, and for directing that sexual assault patients be given priority to be treated as emergency cases. The Office of the Assistant Secretary of Defense for Health Affairs is led by medical professionals and, among other things, exercises authority, direction, and control over DOD medical policy and develops policies, procedures, and standards that govern the management of DOD health and medical programs.[24] The office, in coordination with the Secretaries of the Military Departments, is also charged with developing policies, standards, and procedures for things such as mental health evaluations and treatment and standards to ensure effective and efficient results through the approved joint processes for medical capabilities integration and clinical standardization.

Each military service has established a sexual assault prevention and response office that is responsible for overseeing and managing the service's sexual assault program.[25] Each military service provides sexual assault-specific guidance, as well as standard operating and reporting procedures for responding to alleged sexual assault incidents. Further, DOD's directive requires the military services to establish sexual assault response coordinator positions and notes that at the services' discretion, these positions may be staffed by members of the military or civilian employees.[26] Sexual assault response coordinators are generally responsible for implementing their respective services' sexual assault prevention and response programs, including coordinating the response to and reporting of sexual assault incidents at an installation or within a geographic area. According to DOD's instruction, commanders, supervisors, and managers at all levels are responsible for the effective implementation of both the policy and the program.[27] Other responders include victim advocates, judge advocates, medical and mental health providers, criminal investigative personnel, law-enforcement personnel, and chaplains.

Department of Veterans Affairs Role in Treating Servicemembers Who Were Sexually Assaulted

The Department of Veterans Affairs (VA) assists veterans who experience physical and mental health conditions associated with military sexual trauma after they leave the military. Military sexual trauma is the term used by VA to refer to experiences of sexual assault or repeated, threatening sexual harassment that a veteran experienced during his or her military service. The VA's Veterans Health Administration has a range of outpatient, inpatient, and residential services available to assist veterans in their recovery from military sexual trauma. According to VA policy, every VA health-care facility has a designated military sexual-trauma coordinator who serves as a contact person for related issues and can assist veterans in finding and accessing VA services and programs. Further, VA policy specifies that all veterans seen in VA health-care settings be asked if they experienced military sexual trauma.

DOD Has Taken Steps to Generally Address Sexual Assault but Has Not Used Data on Male Victims to Inform Program Development

Since establishing its sexual assault prevention and response program in 2005, DOD has undertaken a variety of actions to prevent and respond to incidents of sexual assault, including the development of policies and procedures for the department's sexual assault prevention and response program. According to SAPRO officials, these initiatives are largely "gender neutral" or based on an approach that DOD believes serves male and female servicemembers equally well. During this review, DOD began to take steps to address male needs more specifically, such as starting to develop plans to improve male victim reporting and enhance efforts to encourage male victims to seek assistance. However, although it has collected various data and begun to establish methods of measuring program success overall, DOD has not established a plan to use this information to inform program decisions about how to focus and prioritize its efforts.

DOD Officials Identify Approach to Sexual Assault Prevention and Response as Largely Gender Neutral

Since 2005, DOD has undertaken a variety of initiatives, including the development of policies and procedures, to prevent and respond to incidents of sexual assault that involve U.S. servicemembers. According to SAPRO officials, these initiatives are largely "gender neutral," or generally applicable to all servicemembers, and they cited two primary reasons that the department believes this approach serves male and female servicemembers equally well. First, officials stated that this is not a crime that affects just one gender; rather, both males and females can be victims of sexual assault. This is demonstrated by the reports of sexual assaults, both restricted and unrestricted, filed with the department by both males and females. To illustrate, in fiscal year 2014, according to SAPRO, 1,180 male servicemembers and 4,104 female servicemembers filed reports of sexual assault. Figure 1 shows the reported number of servicemember sexual assault victims, by gender, for fiscal years 2008 through 2014.

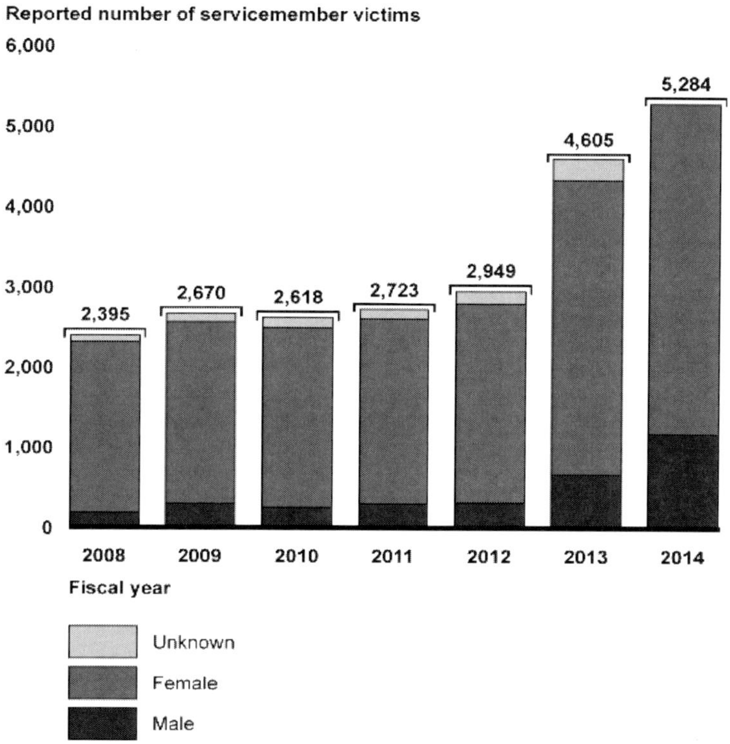

Source: GAO analysis of Department of Defense (DOD) data. I GAO-15-284.

Note: The figure includes both restricted and unrestricted reports of sexual assault. Because of the confidential nature of restricted reports, we are limited in our ability to assess the quality of these data. However, these data are the responsibility of Sexual Assault Response Coordinators, who manage and report on individual cases to their local installation commands, which reduces the likelihood of significant errors in the data. In addition, because for fiscal years 2008 through 2013 DOD's Sexual Assault Prevention and Response Office (SAPRO) did not collect information on the gender of victims converting reports from restricted to unrestricted, we calculated the minimum number of males and females that could have reported in each of these years and categorized the remainder as unknown.

Figure 1. Reported Servicemember Sexual Assault Victims in Fiscal Years 2008 through 2014.

As figure 1 shows, the number of reported servicemember sexual assault victims has more than doubled since fiscal year 2008. Specifically, in fiscal year 2014 DOD reported that a total of 5,284 servicemember victims were identified in a restricted or unrestricted report of sexual assault, compared with 4,605 the prior fiscal year and 2,395 in fiscal year 2008. According to our analysis of DOD's data, 22 percent of the victims in fiscal year 2014 were male, whereas at least 14 percent of the victims the prior fiscal year were male and at least 8 percent of the victims in fiscal year 2008 were male.

Second, SAPRO officials stated that servicemembers, regardless of their gender, experience similar challenges when deciding whether to report being sexually assaulted. In particular, they stated that the hierarchical nature of the military may inhibit the willingness of servicemember victims to seek care—even with the option to do so confidentially under restricted reporting. For example, the majority of the males we spoke with who were sexually assaulted while serving in the military[28] said that they did not trust their chains of command when it came to reporting a sexual assault.[29] For example, one said he did not report his assault because he was concerned about jeopardizing his retirement from the service. Another male victim said it would be preferable to report to an outside authority even if the assault occurred on base. Further, we administered surveys to 122 randomly selected male servicemembers during the course of our visits, and 17 said they would have reservations about reporting unwanted sexual contact and 87 said that they believe that other male servicemembers may have reservations about reporting any unwanted sexual contact.[30] Of those who said that they believe others would have reservations reporting an unwanted sexual contact, we asked them to describe what those reservations might be. Reservations that servicemembers believed others might have varied among individuals. The most commonly cited reservations[31] included: (1) feelings of shame, embarrassment, humiliation, or blaming of oneself; (2) fear of being judged by others, including fear of being seen as weak or less of a man; (3) fear of not fitting in; and (4) fear of the repercussions for reporting. For example, 23 listed fear of repercussions from their chain of command, including the potential for a sexual assault victim to be prosecuted for collateral misconduct such as underage drinking or adultery[32] that may have occurred in conjunction with the alleged sexual assault and fear that reporting the sexual assault would have an adverse effect on the individual's career. Further, servicemembers also cited reservations that only servicemembers may have. For example, 8 of the 87 male servicemembers cited the military's rank structure as a potential obstacle to reporting, especially if the alleged perpetrator was of a higher rank. These challenges are consistent with those noted in our August 2008 report on sexual assault in the military[33] as well as some of the reporting barriers discussed in the June 2014 report of the Response Systems to Adult Sexual Assault Crimes Panel.[34]

DOD Has Not Used Data on Male Victims to Inform Its Sexual Assault Prevention and Response Efforts

As noted previously, DOD has implemented a mostly gender-neutral sexual assault prevention and response program because it believes that this approach serves both males and females equally well. However, our analysis of DOD's data on reported sexual assault incidents and prevalence estimates show that male servicemembers report sexual assaults at statistically significantly lower rates than do female servicemembers, and we found that the department has not used this information to inform program priorities. Leading practices for results-oriented management have shown that data-driven decision making leads to better results. Further, agencies can use performance information to identify problems or weaknesses in programs, to try to identify factors causing the problems, and to modify a service or process to try to address problems.[35] While DOD has used some of its available data to shape its program—for example, focusing on female victims because females constitute the majority of those reporting sexual assaults—it has not established a plan for how it will consider all the data it collects on all victims when making decisions about program development.

DOD collects a variety of data on reported incidents of sexual assault involving servicemembers and, among other things, since 2008 has reported on the gender of sexual assault victims who file both restricted and unrestricted reports with the department. DOD also collects data through its Workplace and Gender Relations Survey of Active Duty Members [36] that it uses to estimate the prevalence of unwanted sexual contact for both male and female servicemembers.[37] Taken together, these data are used to calculate one of the measures that DOD uses to assess program effectiveness, which it determines by calculating the gap between the number of servicemembers who reported and the total number of servicemembers who are estimated to have experienced unwanted sexual contact. DOD has used these two data points to support its belief that an increase in sexual assault reports relative to prevalence estimates is positively correlated with a growing level of confidence in the department's response system. However, although overall reporting of sexual assaults has increased in recent years, a statistically significant difference remains between the proportion of males reporting sexual assaults relative to prevalence estimates (of both unwanted sexual contact and sexual assault) and the proportion of females doing so.

In its comparison of reported sexual assaults and estimated prevalence of unwanted sexual contact, DOD found that female servicemembers report sexual assaults at higher rates than men do relative to DOD's prevalence estimates of unwanted sexual contact, which, based on the department's aforementioned belief, suggests that male victims of sexual assault may not have a similar level of confidence as do female victims in the process of reporting a sexual assault within the department. Specifically, officials determined that in each of fiscal years 2010 and 2012, of those active-duty males estimated to have experienced unwanted sexual contact, about 3 percent reported a sexual assault to DOD. At the same time, officials found that for fiscal year 2010, of those active-duty women estimated to have experienced unwanted sexual contact, about 26 percent reported a sexual assault to DOD, and for fiscal year 2012, the figure was 20 percent. Despite this finding, DOD has not used these data to inform program decision making. Furthermore, DOD has not developed a plan that articulates, for example, the types of data, and analyses of these data, that would be used to inform program development, including allocation of resources and areas of program focus.

We have previously reported on DOD's collection of sexual assault incident data and twice recommended actions that could be used to drive program decision making. For example, in August 2008, we reported that DOD was not collecting installation-level data on sexual assault incidents and recommended that doing so could help to identify installations or units where additional training and resources to prevent sexual assaults may be needed.[38] In February 2010, we similarly reported that the oversight framework for DOD's sexual assault prevention and response program did not identify how program results related to its budgeting of resources and recommended that such a link be established.[39] While DOD has addressed the specifics of these two recommendations, it has not developed a plan to identify and institutionalize how it would use the data it collects to inform program decision making. Such a plan could show which of DOD's various sets of data or measures of program performance would inform the development of focus areas, such as a focus on male victims, and what weight those data or measures would be given in making such decisions relative to each other. For example, a plan could outline how a regular analysis of the rates of reporting of sexual assaults versus prevalence of sexual assaults by both males and females would inform the emphasis on specific genders in DOD's prevention and response efforts.

Our analysis of DOD data also indicated that the proportion of males who experienced unwanted sexual contact relative to those who reported it is significantly lower than the proportion of females who reported for fiscal years 2010 and 2012. This difference is statistically significant. We also reached the same conclusion using fiscal year 2014 data provided by DOD. Specifically, based on our analysis of DOD's fiscal year 2014 sexual assault reports and the results from the 2014 Military Workplace Study conducted by RAND, we estimated that—at most—13 percent of males reported their sexual assaults relative to the estimated prevalence of sexual assault, compared to at least 40 percent of females reporting their sexual assaults relative to the estimated prevalence of sexual assault.[40]

We recognize that it is impossible to determine the precise number of sexual assaults involving servicemembers, and that studies suggest sexual assaults are generally underreported in the United States. However, unlike the male population outside of DOD, men constitute 85 percent of the military's active-duty force, and SAPRO officials noted that there may be as many or more men as there are women experiencing sexual assault in the military. Further, in both the 2009 and 2013 versions of its Sexual Assault Prevention and Response Strategic Plan, DOD identified increasing the number and percentage of sexual assaults reported as one of the department's priorities.[41] Also, DOD's 2008 sexual assault prevention strategy discussed males who are sexually assaulted, noting that males are less likely to report sexual assaults than females.

SAPRO officials stated that they have focused the program on females because females constitute the overwhelming majority of those filing reports of sexual assault and because they are at a higher risk of being sexually assaulted based on the higher estimated prevalence rates of unwanted sexual contact for women. Officials from one military service similarly acknowledged that the department's execution of its sexual assault prevention and response program has traditionally been skewed toward females.

DOD has recently started to take steps to address incidents of male servicemembers being sexually assaulted. For example, in a May 2014 memorandum accompanying the department's April 2014 sexual assault prevention strategy, the Secretary of Defense directed the military services to implement methods that encourage male sexual assault victims to report and to seek care, and required that an implementation plan for these methods be submitted by January 2015.[42] To support these efforts the Marine Corps in

September 2014 hosted an interservice working-group meeting which concluded that additional efforts were needed to create a reporting process more accommodating to male victims of sexual assault. An official of the Marine Corps' Sexual Assault Prevention and Response program said the service's plan would (1) link males to the DOD Safe Helpline website and local support services; (2) consider outreach efforts; (3) include awareness training for dealing with males who experienced sexual assault; and (4) use available survey data and consider obtaining input from males who report sexual assault in a focus-group setting to increase understanding and methods of outreach.

An official of the Air Force's Sexual Assault Prevention and Response program stated that the Air Force implementation plan includes working with the other military services through the Marine Corps' working group; incorporating the issue of male victims into a week-long Sexual Assault Prevention Summit in January 2015 that will address the topic and include a working group of male victims; continuing to engage subject-matter experts on sexual violence against males; and hiring a full-time prevention expert with a background in sexual assault prevention research. An official of the Navy's Sexual Assault Prevention and Response program stated that the Navy's planning is in the early stages and did not provide additional detail on the planning process or goals, and an official of the Army's Sexual Harassment/Assault Response and Prevention program stated the service is incorporating additional content on male victims into its sexual assault prevention training, including new videos that include male victims or are gender neutral. Each of the services provided their implementation plans to DOD in January 2015, and as of March 2015 the department was reviewing the plans.

We acknowledge the positive steps that the services are starting to take in response to sexual assaults of male servicemembers, but the majority of DOD's efforts still remain focused around females as the primary sexual assault victims, which only partially reflects the data on sexual assault that DOD has collected and analyzed. SAPRO officials said they have focused the sexual assault prevention and response program mainly on female victims because females have constituted the majority of those reporting sexual assaults, and additionally, that until recently DOD leadership was not comfortable raising male victims as an area of focus. However, establishing a plan for data-driven decision making that details how DOD's various data, and analyses of these data, would inform program development would institutionalize this practice and reduce the extent to which program decisions are made based on cultural norms and expectations, such as the tendency to view females as the primary victims of sexual assault. Without a plan for data-driven decision making, DOD runs the risk of not focusing and prioritizing its efforts as appropriate to address the needs of male servicemember victims.

DOD Offers Health Care to All Sexual Assault Victims, but Has Not Systematically Evaluated and Provided Guidance on Gender-Specific Health-Care Needs

DOD has taken a variety of steps to provide and to improve the availability of medical and mental health care for all victims of sexual assault, regardless of their gender. Specifically, DOD's directive and instruction on the prevention of and response to sexual assault specify that the department's programs shall provide gender-responsive care that acknowledges and is sensitive to gender differences and gender-specific issues. However, although DOD entities have conducted some evaluations to determine whether females have specific needs, the Office of the Assistant Secretary of Defense for Health Affairs has not systematically evaluated, using various available sources of information, the extent to which either male or female victims of sexual assault have any gender-specific needs or whether the department's current care is sufficiently developed to ensure that such needs are met. Furthermore, although SAPRO officials told us that they have in-house expertise that includes experience with and knowledge of research on male sexual assault victims, and some military-service care providers have experience with male sexual assault victims, the Office of the Assistant Secretary of Defense for Health Affairs has not provided guidance throughout the department on gender-specific care in order to leverage this expertise so as to help its providers to optimize their treatment of male victims.

Medical and Mental Health Care Is Available to All Servicemembers Who Are Sexually Assaulted, Regardless of Their Gender

The Ronald W. Reagan National Defense Authorization Act for Fiscal Year 2005 directed DOD to develop a comprehensive policy on the prevention of and response to sexual assaults involving members of the armed forces.[43] In accordance with this requirement, DOD published a directive in October 2005 that specifies, among other things, the various types of care available to servicemembers in the aftermath of a sexual assault.[44] For example, DOD's directive specifies that victims of sexual assault shall receive timely access to comprehensive medical treatment and that services consist of emergency medical care and the offer of a sexual assault forensic examination consistent with the Department of Justice protocol.[45] In June 2006, DOD issued an instruction that provided guidance on, among other things, providing medical care to sexual assault victims, such as requiring that military treatment facilities provide sexual assault forensic exams and notifying a sexual assault response coordinator or victim advocate when treatment for sexual assault is sought at a military treatment facility.[46]

In addition to issuing the directive and instruction, DOD has taken a variety of steps to improve servicemembers' access to medical and mental health care after a sexual assault. For example, in April 2011, DOD launched Safe Helpline,[47] which includes a website and online and telephone helplines, among other things, as a crisis support service for servicemember sexual assault victims. The Safe Helpline website includes a list of Frequently Asked Questions on issues specific to male sexual assault victims. Figure 2 shows the male survivors information page of DOD's Safe Helpline website.

Additionally, in January 2012, the department revised its directive on the sexual assault prevention and response program to require that sexual assault victims be treated as emergency cases in military treatment facilities, regardless of the presence of apparent injuries.[48] In January 2013, we found that DOD had taken steps to address the provision of medical and mental health care for servicemembers who are sexually assaulted, but several factors affected the extent to which this care is available. These included that the branch of military service and the operational uncertainties of a deployed environment could affect the ready availability of medical and mental health-care services for sexual assault victims, and in some cases care was affected because military health-care providers did not have a consistent understanding of their responsibilities in caring for sexual assault victims who make restricted reports of sexual assault.[49] We had recommended that the Assistant Secretary of Defense for Health Affairs develop and implement guidance on the provision of care that specifies providers' responsibilities to respond to and care for sexual assault victims. DOD did not concur with this recommendation and did not clearly explain why in its response to our report, but subsequently included such guidance in its instruction on the sexual assault prevention and response program. Since that time, DOD has taken steps to increase its capacity to provide medical services related to sexual assault, such as revising its instruction on the sexual assault prevention and response program to include information on health-care provider procedures.

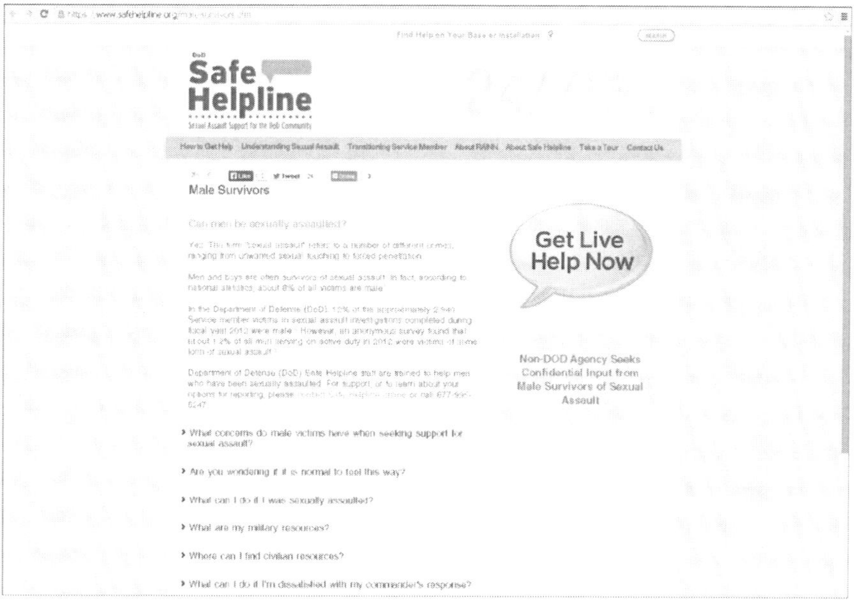

Source: Department of Defense (DOD). I GAO-15-284.

Figure 2. Safe Helpline Male Survivors Page.

Existing Research and Expertise Suggest That Males Have Specific Needs and Responses to Sexual Assault

During the course of this review, we spoke with two clinicians at the VA's Center for Sexual Trauma Services[50] in Bay Pines, Florida who have extensive experience working with male sexual assault victims. Both clinicians told us that based on their research and personal experience, male victims are more likely than women to manifest their trauma externally through problems with behavioral control, interpersonal relationships, and sexual dysfunction. Further, because of such issues, the clinicians suggested that men may be more likely to avoid reporting or seeking treatment for the trauma while in the military, and they emphasized the need for additional research on gender-specific symptom profiles and characteristics, barriers to disclosure, and treatment outcomes for victims of military sexual trauma. We also reviewed a number of academic studies, published from January 2008 through September 2014 that identified key distinctions in how males and females respond as victims of sexual assault and noted the importance of tailoring the response to meet those needs.[51] For example:

- One study stated that, while females are also hesitant to report sexual assault, males' reluctance may be exacerbated by a sense of shame about not being in control and taking care of matters themselves, which are norms of masculinity.[52]
- Another study stated that sexual assault can lead to confusion over sex roles as well as sexual orientation for heterosexual males and to feelings of self-blame and self-loathing in homosexual males.[53]
- In a study on sex differences in exposure to trauma and the development of post-traumatic stress disorder after interpersonal assault, the study noted that, in its small sample, males endorsed more feelings of anger directed inward while females endorsed more guilt thoughts.[54]
- Another study said that the effect of assault on sense of sexuality and identity, especially masculinity, may be stronger for males who are more likely to repress the event or avoid disclosure.[55]
- One article stated that male sexual assault victims have fewer resources and greater stigma when compared to female sexual assault victims.[56]

We also reviewed studies on the effectiveness of treatment for male victims of sexual assault. For example, in a 2008 study, researchers found that psychological symptoms in men appear to be more persistent and resistant to treatment after military sexual trauma[57] than in women,[58] and researchers in a 2013 study similarly observed more sustained gains from treatment in women survivors than in men.[59]

DOD Has Not Systematically Evaluated Gender-Specific Health-Care Needs for Sexual Assault Victims

DOD's directive and instruction on the prevention of and response to sexual assault specify that its programs shall provide gender-responsive care that acknowledges and is sensitive to gender differences and gender-specific issues. However, neither document provides further details about the provision of gender-specific care, and therefore does not provide guidance to care providers on considerations for providing male sexual assault victims with gender-responsive care. As we reported in January 2013, DOD and service officials have stated that although there may be some gender differences for particular diagnoses, behavior health-care services such as mental health care are not gender-specific, and the treatment of servicemembers' behavioral health-care needs and the availability of services to meet those needs do not vary based on gender.[60] Further, the Office of the Assistant Secretary of Defense for Health Affairs—the organization responsible for ensuring the effective execution of the department's medical mission—has not developed guidance that more specifically identifies the gender-specific issues and the gender-responsive care noted in DOD's sexual assault prevention and response policies.

Notwithstanding the direction to provide gender-responsive care, DOD has not standardized throughout the department the provision of gender-responsive care for male sexual assault victims because its Office of the Assistant Secretary of Defense for Health Affairs has not systematically evaluated the extent to which male victims have gender-specific medical and mental health-care needs and provided guidance on this assessment to care providers throughout the department. Leading practices for program evaluation have shown that systematic evaluation of programs is key to identifying and addressing problems.[61] In this case, a systematic evaluation of gender-specific needs could use research methods to synthesize available information on gender-specific needs. Furthermore, as discussed below, DOD studies and officials indicate that military culture can foster standards of behavior that may either encourage or deter sexual assault. The military environment, which is unique and remains overwhelmingly male, gives DOD a distinct opportunity to both evaluate and provide guidance on treatment for male sexual assault victims.

Various DOD entities have conducted some evaluations to determine whether females, including those who are sexually assaulted, have any gender-specific needs. For example, the Army Surgeon General's office issued a white paper in 2011 that focused on female-specific concerns about topics that included reporting a sexual assault and inadequate physical-security measures during deployment. [62] Further, a January 2013 study contracted by the U.S. Army Medical Research and Materiel Command addressed health-care delivery needs of women who are sexually assaulted during military service and of women exposed to combat.[63] Another 2013 study, funded by a DOD medical research program, examined the relationship between deployment and sexual assault and harassment in female servicemembers, recognizing its effects on physical and mental health.[64] However, these studies were not products of a department-wide effort that included the cooperation with and endorsement of each military service's surgeon general, and therefore do not represent the conclusions of the department as a whole. DOD also has not systematically evaluated whether male victims of sexual assault have any gender-specific needs.

Mental health-care professionals from the military services and SAPRO officials said that the department employs evidence-based mental healthcare treatment where practitioners draw on research, theory, and practical experience to treat the individual needs of each client and that this approach would capture any gender-related issues. However, the levels of experience with male sexual assault victims that medical and mental health-care providers reported to us varied, as some had extensive experience and others little or no experience. Additionally, DOD has previously identified that more research is needed on the specific needs of male victims of sexual assault. For example, in August 2008, DOD's Office of the Assistant Secretary of Defense for Health Affairs published findings from a congressionally mandated review of gender-specific mental health needs and treatment. In that report, the Assistant Secretary noted, and the military services agreed, that there was a need for additional research on the gender-specific needs of servicemembers. 65 Further, DOD's 2008 sexual assault prevention strategy, though superseded by a revised strategy that was published in 2014, noted the importance of providing those within DOD who respond to sexual assault incidents with knowledge about topics such as masculinity and male-on-male sexual assault.[66] While the department has acknowledged that more information is needed on the gender-specific needs of male servicemembers who are sexually assaulted, DOD has not taken steps to systematically identify these needs.

DOD employs medical and mental health providers and works with subject-matter experts, some of whom have professional experience working with males who have been sexually assaulted. However, DOD is missing opportunities to more effectively address the issue of male victims of sexual assault because its Office of the Assistant Secretary of Defense for Health Affairs has not effectively leveraged the expertise of these individuals who work in various organizations across, as well as outside, DOD, by using this expertise to provide guidance to care providers across the department on gender-specific needs of sexual assault victims. Leading practices for collaboration call for organizations to leverage each others' resources and thereby obtain additional benefits that would not have been available if they were working separately. [67] In addition, federal internal-control standards state that information should be communicated to management and others within an organization who need it in a form and time frame that enables them to carry out their responsibilities.[68] Although some of the military medical and mental health-care providers we met with during our review had limited or no experience working with male sexual assault victims, others provided insights based on their professional experience treating the trauma experienced by male victims of sexual assault and observing the types of care to which they most effectively respond. Following those meetings, we compared the various observations made and identified two themes most frequently identified by these experts about the trauma experienced by male victims in the aftermath of a sexual assault.

- *Male Victims Experience Shame and Question Masculinity.* Care providers at several installations we visited said that male sexual assault victims typically experience shame and embarrassment and face stigma that the assault portrays them as weak and not masculine. Four providers further suggested that these gender-specific views come from cultural norms and stereotypes. Specifically, female sexual assault victims are more likely to open up about being assaulted because they are conditioned to be aware—and thus are more accepting—that they are vulnerable. Conversely, males do not typically have a similar awareness of susceptibility and thus may be more likely to blame themselves for being assaulted.
- *Male Victims Face Questions about Their Sexuality.* Providers also told us that, following an assault, heterosexual male victims may face questions about their sexuality. For example, providers stated that male victims may misunderstand physical responses that they experienced during the assault, and in some cases may conclude that they subconsciously "wanted it" and "invited" the attack.

While the knowledge and experience of these providers internal to DOD echo the findings of those outside the department as demonstrated by our literature review and conversations with outside experts, DOD's Office of the Assistant Secretary of Defense for Health Affairs has not used this experience, among other sources of information, to provide guidance for use by all care providers within the department specifically on providing care to male victims.

Leveraging its internal experience, as well as drawing on outside expertise and research and the research the department has begun to conduct on male victims, to inform guidance for care providers could strengthen the provision of care throughout the department for male sexual assault victims.

While DOD's Office of the Assistant Secretary of Defense for Health Affairs has not systematically evaluated male-specific medical and mental health-care needs for sexual assault victims, the department has begun to take steps that could yield valuable information on, among other things, whether male victims of sexual assault have any gender-specific needs. Specifically, DOD's April 2014 sexual assault prevention strategy states that DOD will conduct research to better understand the situations that give rise to male victimization and the special needs that male sexual assault survivors may have.[69] SAPRO officials said that to carry this out, the department began collecting information about servicemember experiences of sexual assault, with an increased focus on male servicemembers, in its 2014 Military Workplace Study conducted by the RAND Corporation. The full survey results are due to DOD in early 2015 and, once fully analyzed by SAPRO officials, these survey results may contribute to a better understanding of male servicemember needs. However, by themselves these survey results will not yield a full picture of available information, which could include existing research on gender differences and the knowledge of clinicians experienced in working with male sexual assault victims, whereas a systematic evaluation would include a full range of available information, such as existing research, the views of experts both within and outside DOD, existing survey information, and any other available sources. DOD's Office of the Assistant Secretary of Defense for Health Affairs has not systematically evaluated the extent to which there are gender-specific needs of sexual assault victims, and in turn has not provided guidance on gender-specific needs to care providers, because, according to officials, its stated practice of using evidence-based treatment would capture any gender-specific issues. However, absent a systematic evaluation of the extent of such gender-specific needs and sharing the results, including any care regimen that might best meet those needs, with care providers throughout the department, the Office of the Assistant Secretary of Defense for Health Affairs may be limited in the extent to which it can help care providers throughout the department, including those with less or no experience with male victims, to meet any gender-specific needs that sexual assault victims may have.

MILITARY CULTURE CAN POSE CHALLENGES FOR MALE VICTIMS, BUT DOD HAS NOT TAKEN KEY STEPS NEEDED TO MITIGATE THESE ISSUES

Military culture helps foster standards of behavior that, depending on the leadership, can cultivate an environment that encourages or deters behavior that can lead to sexual assault and whether a victim chooses to report an incident, according to DOD reports and strategies and officials with whom we spoke. The same evidence suggests that military culture and its high regard for masculine traits such as strength and self-reliance can be a particularly potent influence on how male servicemembers respond to issues such as sexual assault. Leading practices for achieving results-oriented cultures and effecting change within organizations have shown that key practices for achieving these ends include establishing performance goals and measuring progress toward them, communicating goals and values, and training employees as a means to effect the desired change.[70] DOD has stated that a culture change is needed, throughout the department, on its approach to addressing the incidence of sexual assault. However, several key issues pose challenges to DOD's ability to achieve the necessary change in its culture with regard to male victims. First, DOD has not clearly articulated goals related to male sexual assault victims nor has it identified performance measures that would tie such goals to specific results. Second, DOD has not effectively articulated its support of male victims in the materials it uses to communicate its efforts to prevent and respond to sexual assault. Third, the military services' sexual assault prevention and response training material does not address the incidence of sexual assault of males in a way that effectively raises awareness of the issue or conveys the department's intended support for male victims.

Military Culture Can Affect Sexual Assault and Create Particular Vulnerabilities in Male Servicemembers

Military culture can play an important role in building and maintaining a cohesive environment that discourages sexual assault. According to a DOD task force on sexual assault in the military services, military culture helps foster standards of behavior that are the building blocks of unit cohesion and esprit de corps.[71] For example, each military service incorporates concepts related to unit cohesion in its sexual assault prevention and response training that encourage servicemembers to intervene when they witness behavior that could lead to a sexual assault. Known as “bystander intervention,” this training is designed to motivate and empower servicemembers to intervene when they witness behavior that is inappropriate and inconsistent with the military’s core values. Both headquarters-level and installation service officials as well as outside experts described the positive effect that unit cohesion can have, such as servicemembers holding each other accountable for their actions; picking up the slack for a servicemember who may be hurt, injured, or have to attend appointments; and watching out for fellow servicemembers.

At the same time, aspects of military culture may pose challenges for DOD’s sexual assault prevention and response efforts, including the stigma attached to sexual assault and the hierarchical nature of the military. For example, in its April 2014 sexual assault prevention strategy, 72 DOD noted that servicemembers are particularly affected by the stigma associated with reporting a sexual assault while serving in the military. Specifically, DOD noted that the hierarchical nature of the military presents opportunities for those in positions of authority to sexually coerce subordinates, and the general military ideals of confidence, decisiveness, and strength may discourage a victim from reporting a sexual assault out of fear that they may be labeled as weak. In 2009, the Defense Task Force on Sexual Assault in the Military Services published a report that similarly stated that elements of unit cohesion could dissuade victims from reporting a sexual assault. The task force further noted that this apprehension is especially pronounced when victims and their alleged assailants are in the same unit because victims fear being disbelieved, judged, or ostracized by coworkers and not being considered a member of the team.[73]

Further, evidence suggests that military culture can be a particularly potent influence on how male servicemembers respond to issues such as sexual assault. We found that gender has played a significant role in defining a servicemember’s position and the opportunities that are available to him or her in the U.S. military, and such distinctions have been a catalyst for the long-standing debate over the role of and occupations open to female servicemembers.[74] While our prior work has found that DOD has made progress over the years to lessen the role that gender plays in its treatment of females, subject-matter experts and mental health-care providers we interviewed said that these same traditional gender stereotypes can make it particularly difficult for males to report that they were sexually assaulted. For example, the 2009 report of the Defense Task Force on Sexual Assault in the Military Services noted that male victims of sexual assault contend with myths of male strength and sexuality which lead many to believe that "real" men do not get raped and that males raped by another man must be homosexual. These traits are heightened in the military environment that, according to DOD's April 2014 sexual assault prevention strategy, idealizes confidence, decisiveness, and strength, and that until 2011, had a policy of initiating separation of servicemembers who committed homosexual acts.[75] SAPRO officials similarly said that information drawn from their interactions with male victims indicates that some male victims feared being labeled as either weak or homosexual. Specifically, these officials noted that the military is a highly masculine environment where feelings of helplessness and powerlessness are not acceptable.

In addition to the officials with whom we spoke, 87 of the 122 randomly selected male servicemembers who participated in our interviewer-administered surveys said that they believe that others may have reservations reporting any unwanted sexual contact. We asked those who said that they believe others would have reservations reporting an unwanted sexual contact to describe what those reservations might be. As noted earlier, fear of being judged by others—particularly if it led to questions about their masculinity or sexual orientation—was among the most frequent. Survey participants also cited the fear of not having the support of their leadership and colleagues as another reason that a male servicemember may not report that he was a victim of sexual assault. Our interviews with 12 males who were sexually assaulted while serving in the military echoed these concerns. Specifically, 6 of the 12 male victims we interviewed said they did not report the assault due to a belief that there would be a negative outcome if they reported it. For example, one male victim said that military culture encourages men to see themselves as dominant males and leaders, and that being sexually assaulted makes you feel like you are less than a man, helpless and weak, and stated that he had previously seen other sexual assault victims be treated badly after reporting an assault.

Commanders with whom we met stated their support for the military's sexual assault prevention and response program, and noted that they face challenges in responding to the behavior of their subordinates and deciding how to respond appropriately to sexual assault cases in their units. However, some other military officials at each installation we visited described varying levels of support from their commanders on the issue of male victims of sexual assault. While officials at each installation we visited and servicemembers we interviewed stated that their commanders were supportive of the sexual assault prevention and response program, other officials at each installation provided examples of unsupportive behavior, particularly with regard to male victims. For example, sexual assault response coordinators at one installation said that they have overheard officers, while in the presence of junior military personnel, make derogatory comments and express their disbelief that males could be raped. Victim advocates at two installations said that, based on their experience in the military, they believed that some commanders chose not to address hazing-type incidents that could have been sexual assault. Installation officials at each installation we visited also reported other unsupportive behaviors by some commanders, such as seeking excessive details about victims, victim blaming, and not supporting servicemembers in attending medical and mental health appointments. While these reported experiences are not generalizable to commanders throughout the department, they suggest that some challenges remain to gaining the full support of all commanders for DOD's efforts to address sexual assaults of male servicemembers.

DOD Has Not Identified Program Goals and Measures Specific to the Incidence of Sexual Assault of Male Servicemembers

According to leading practices for organizational change, because culture change or transformation entails fundamental and often radical change, strong and inspirational leadership is indispensable.[76] Leading practices also establish that it is important for senior officials to articulate and live by organizational values and beliefs to demonstrate to employees that top management is committed to making permanent cultural changes.[77] It is also important for top leadership to provide a clear, consistent rationale that brings together the originating components behind a single mission to guide the transformation and bridge the differences in leadership and management styles among the originating components. Also, articulating this succinct and compelling reason for change helps employees, customers, and stakeholders understand the expected outcomes of the transformation and engenders not only their cooperation, but also their ownership of these outcomes. Therefore, it is key that top leadership define and articulate a succinct and compelling reason for change. Leading practices for successful transformation efforts show that a key practice is establishing a coherent mission and integrating strategic goals to guide the transformation.[78] Developing, communicating, and constantly reinforcing the mission and strategic goals give employees a sense of what the organization intends to accomplish. Therefore, it is important for the mission and strategic goals of a transformed organization to become the focus of the transformation, define the culture, and serve as the vehicle for employees to unite and rally around.[79] While DOD has made progress with the prevention of and response to sexual assault in the military generally, the department's top leadership has recently begun to take steps addressing male victims specifically.

Since the establishment of DOD's sexual assault prevention and response program in 2005, there has been demonstrated growth in the commitment and involvement of top DOD leadership to generally prevent and respond to sexual assault in the military. In April 2012, then Secretary of Defense Leon Panetta said that sexual assault has no place in DOD. In May 2012, for the first time, the Joint Chiefs of Staff provided strategic direction to the joint force on the prevention of and response to sexual assault. Further, beginning in 2013, both DOD's strategic plan and its strategy for preventing sexual assault were accompanied by memorandums from the Secretary of Defense directing that the department take various specific actions to address sexual assault. Also, the National Defense Authorization Act for Fiscal Year 2012 mandated that the Director position at SAPRO be elevated and filled by either a general/flag officer or a Senior Executive Service civilian DOD employee. Since that change, DOD has filled this position with a general officer at the Major General level. However, since 2011 the Director's position has been filled by three different general officers, and in that same period there have been three different Secretaries of Defense, further reducing continuity.

DOD leadership has stated that a culture change is needed throughout the department to effectively address sexual assaults of male service members. For example, in 2008, DOD published a sexual assault prevention strategy in which it concluded that the department would need to change aspects of its culture in order to effectively implement a program to prevent sexual assault.[80] Specifically, DOD highlighted that it would need to address the "unofficial" culture that is defined by exaggerated characteristics of stereotypical masculinity, among other things, and is linked to values and customs that perpetuate rape. In its April 2013 sexual assault prevention and response strategic plan, DOD stated that underpinning its efforts was the need for enduring culture change. These efforts included a variety of specific tasks, such as enhancing training and conducting command-climate surveys. Additionally, in the fiscal year 2013 *Department of Defense Annual Report on Sexual Assault in the Military*, DOD added that the end state of its prevention efforts was that the "cultural imperatives" of mutual respect and trust, professional values, and team commitment would be reinforced to create an environment where sexual assault was not tolerated, condoned, or ignored.[81]

DOD's report also identified the need to emphasize positive aspects of military culture, that include mutual respect, trust, and professionalism to achieve enduring culture change on issues such as the department's efforts to address sexual assaults of male servicemembers. In May 2014, the Secretary of Defense directed that to advance and sustain an appropriate culture for combating sexual assault, the military departments would develop plans to update and integrate programs for leaders and service members to address healthy relationships, active bystander intervention, social courage, and core values supporting the establishment of mutual respect. However, until 2014, none of these initiatives specifically aimed to address issues surrounding male sexual assault victims.

During this review, DOD began to implement initiatives aimed specifically at addressing the incidence of sexual assault of male servicemembers. As noted previously, in May 2014, in a memo accompanying the department's April 2014 sexual assault prevention strategy, the Secretary of Defense required that the military services implement methods to encourage male sexual assault victims to report and to seek care, and required that an implementation plan for these methods be submitted by January 2015. Also, as noted previously, the 2014 prevention strategy stated that DOD would conduct research to better understand the situations that give rise to male victimization and the special needs that male victims may have. [82] In response to a presidential request, DOD, in November 2014 provided the President with a report on the progress over the prior 3 years of its sexual assault prevention and response program. The report referred to the initiative to increase male victim reporting but did not reference any further initiatives specifically related to male sexual assault victims.

Although DOD has repeatedly identified the need for culture change as well as actions intended to achieve this change, it has not identified goals specifically related to the incidence of sexual assaults of males in its April 2013 strategic plan, its April 2014 prevention strategy, or its November 2014 report to the President on its efforts to address sexual assault in the military. Key practices for implementing organizational transformations include establishing performance goals for which agencies will be held accountable and measuring progress toward these goals.[83]

DOD's program to prevent and respond to sexual assault continues to evolve, and its report to the President included an expanded list of what it called "provisional metrics" on sexual assault. These included measures for which DOD can identify the results by gender, such as the estimated rates of sexual assault as measured in the 2014 Military Workplace Study, as well as rates of bystander intervention indicated in surveys. Although the results of these measures can be shown for both males and females, DOD has not articulated how the results relate to its intended cultural transformation, particularly with regard to male sexual assault victims. According to DOD officials, DOD has not developed clear goals and metrics relating to male victims and included them in its prevention strategy because it has viewed its approach toward its sexual assault prevention and response program as gender neutral and because it has focused its program mainly on female victims. Developing clear goals and associated metrics related to male victims, and articulating them throughout the department—for example, in its next sexual assault prevention strategy—would better position DOD to have a clear path toward achieving the culture change needed and provide it with additional information to assess its progress and determine whether any adjustments are needed in its approach for addressing sexual assault of males in the military.

Primary Communications on Sexual Assault Do Not Portray Male Sexual Assault Victims

Although DOD has recognized the need to address the incidence of male servicemembers being sexually assaulted, it has not aligned how that message is communicated through other forums, such as promotional material, to reflect this recognition. According to leading practices for organizational change, in order to effect desired change, organizations must communicate information about goals, values and beliefs.[84] We examined the primary materials used throughout the department to raise awareness about sexual assault in the military—in particular, posters that appear at military installations. These posters can generate awareness of DOD's sexual assault prevention and response programs among servicemembers as well as convey DOD's intended values regarding sexual assault. However, we generally found that they either did not identify the gender of the perpetrator or the victim, or that they specifically portrayed the male as the perpetrator and the female as the victim.

None of the materials explicitly portrayed a male as a victim of sexual assault. For example, we reviewed 36 Sexual Assault Awareness Month posters developed and used by SAPRO and the military services from fiscal years 2007 through 2014, which encompassed the years of posters available on the SAPRO website at the time we conducted the review in 2014.[85] Figure 3 provides an example of a poster used by each service.

Source: Department of Defense (DOD). | GAO-15-284.

Figure 3. Examples of Sexual Assault Awareness Month Posters.

The Army poster depicts a female soldier who is talking about how she encouraged a friend to report that a "guy went way too far," thus identifying a male as the perpetrator. Although the gender of the victim is not specified, the speaker depicted is female. The quote used in the Marine Corps poster—"So when she told the victim advocate what that guy did to her ..."—clearly depicts that the victim was female and the perpetrator was male. The Air Force poster shows two males and encourages servicemembers to act when "someone inappropriately touches" a fellow servicemember, but it does not clearly identify the gender of a victim or perpetrator. Finally, the Navy Poster includes two male and one female servicemember with the quote "So we reported that guy who wouldn't leave our shipmate alone." The quote clearly depicts a male perpetrator, while the victim's gender is left ambiguous. According to DOD officials, DOD has not clearly depicted male victims in its communications to servicemembers because it has seen its program as gender neutral and because of its focus on female victims. As previously noted, these posters can generate awareness of DOD's sexual assault prevention and response programs among servicemembers as well as convey DOD's intended values regarding sexual assault, such as the need to intervene. However, including more depictions of male victims could further increase awareness of DOD's efforts specifically regarding sexual assaults of males.

DOD's Sexual Assault Prevention and Response Training Includes Limited References to Male Victims of Sexual Assault

Leading practices for organizational change also show that, in order to achieve needed change, organizations must provide training that is aligned with organizational goals and promotes and develops skills related to their desired values and beliefs.[86] DOD's instruction for its sexual assault prevention and response program specifies, among other things, that military and DOD civilian officials at each management level should provide education and training to enable them to prevent and appropriately respond to incidents of sexual assault.[87] The instruction also requires that annual sexual assault prevention and response training use scenario-based, real-life situations to demonstrate the entire cycle of prevention, reporting, response, and accountability procedures.

In accordance with DOD's instruction, each military service annually administers sexual assault prevention and response training. Requiring regular training on sexual assault prevention and response, as DOD does, is a useful tool to increase awareness of DOD's sexual assault programs and convey the department's intended values regarding sexual assault. However, in our review of each service's training material, we found limited information on male victims of sexual assault. For example, we found that most of the services' sexual assault prevention and response training material either generally portrayed sexual assault victims as female, or were gender neutral in the discussion. The following examples further illustrate the extent to which the services' training addresses the sexual victimization of males.

- *Navy train-the-trainer video.* We reviewed a video recording of the Navy's fiscal year 2012 and 2013 training for senior officers to prepare them to administer the training to lower-level officers and very senior enlisted, who in turn would administer the training throughout the fleet. The training was built around a fictional video portraying the sexual assault of a female servicemember by a male servicemember, and included video clips of senior leaders and servicemembers experienced with sexual assault as well as facilitated discussions, including discussion led by a military lawyer. However, the nearly 2- hour training briefly acknowledged the existence of male victims with a few statements such as "it's a devastating crime against males and females" and "it's not just male on female—it's also male on male, female on female." However, no particular examples were presented to support the existence of sexual assault of males, nor were any details discussed about how a case might differ if the victim was a male.
- *Army briefing slides and video.* The briefing slides for the Army's 2014 refresher and pre- and postdeployment training for sexual assault and sexual harassment included five scenarios. Three of these had a male perpetrator and female victim, one did not have a victim or perpetrator, and one involved a female perpetrator and male victim—however, the latter was an example of sexual harassment, not sexual assault. The Army also had separate male and female training videos for new recruits, and the video for males included discussion of both male on male and female on male sexual assault, and a scenario of a female attempting to coerce a male into sex.
- *Air Force briefing slides and videos.* The Air Force's April 2014 sexual assault prevention and response training slides included 12 scenarios.

  Of these, 5 did not identify the gender of victims or perpetrators, and 7 presented female victims and male perpetrators; none presented male victims. We also reviewed 7 Air Force training videos, 4 of which showed female victims, 1 did not specify any victim gender, and 2 of which showed male victims. The videos with male victims showed a servicemember disclosing to a superior officer that he was previously assaulted; it did not provide details as to how the assault occurred or who was the perpetrator. An Air Force training facilitation guide also included a section for the instructor discussing possible differences between males and females as sexual assault victims and differences in the types of disclosures each gender might make during sexual assault discussions, and noted that "men are survivors of sexual assault" in addition to females.

- *Marine Corps videos.* Marine Corps videos that are required for use with its noncommissioned-officer training include a video with servicemembers who were sexually assaulted relating their experiences, including two male victims. Training for junior enlisted servicemembers, however, do not include required videos that depict male victims. The Marine Corps also developed videos to facilitate discussion groups that included depictions of male victims, but these are not required to be used.

We also interviewed a variety of program personnel from each service who similarly identified that the sexual assault prevention and response training currently being used is missing key information that is needed to raise awareness and to effectively counter myths about male victims of sexual assault. For example, sexual assault response coordinators—who themselves administer sexual assault prevention and response training— at each of the four installations we visited said that there is insufficient awareness of the gender-specific challenges that men may encounter as victims of sexual assault, and they noted that generally the training does not depict male victims, and whether or not issues relating to male victims arise in training depends on the trainer. Some of the response coordinators further stated that the lack of training on the sexual victimization of males likely contributes to the underreporting by male servicemembers because it suggests that the department is uncomfortable with discussing the topic. Military mental health-care providers at each of the installations we visited explained that males, unlike females, traditionally are not raised to be aware that they are vulnerable to an attack—including sexual assault—and that they need to take deliberate steps to minimize their exposure to such risk. Therefore, according to these officials as well as sexual assault response coordinators at the installations we visited, training that is almost exclusively based on scenarios that depict males assaulting females can reinforce the commonly-held belief among male victims that they are alone in their experience.

During interviews with 122 randomly selected male servicemembers at the locations we visited, we asked what, if anything, they thought that male servicemembers want from their commands to address sexual assault. Responses varied among individuals, but the top two most frequently cited were (1) support of leadership in which there is zero tolerance for sexual assault and a command climate that encourages reporting, and (2) that their command address sexual assault on males, including the stigma associated with male sexual assault victims, in training. Likewise, 6 of the 12 males we interviewed who were sexually assaulted while in the military identified education and training regarding male victims as an important factor in improving the environment in the military for males who have been sexually assaulted. These observations, when considered in conjunction with our findings, demonstrate that the predominance of female victim–centric training scenarios raises questions about whether servicemembers are fully educated about the incidence of and myths associated with males being sexually assaulted. A more comprehensive discussion during training about male victims of sexual assault could better position DOD and its servicemembers to provide, and male victims to seek, the support that is needed in the aftermath of a sexual assault. DOD officials said that in general, their training has focused on females because they constitute the majority of those filing reports of sexual assault, and because females have higher rates of being sexually assaulted relative to the size of their population.

In addition to the limited information about male victims of sexual assault, our review of the services' training material found that it generally does not discuss activities—such as hazing—that male servicemembers are known to engage in and may actually constitute a sexual assault. DOD's instruction[88] on implementing the sexual assault prevention and response program identifies a variety of training competencies that military personnel are required to complete on the prevention of and response to sexual assault. The instruction also states that annual sexual assault training shall explain the nature of sexual assault in the military environment using scenario-based, real-life situations to demonstrate the entire cycle of prevention, reporting, response, and accountability procedures. However, of the more than 40 examples of the services' sexual assault prevention training materials that we reviewed, we identified three involving incidents that were characterized as hazing and also constituted sexual assault under the UCMJ.

Although hazing and sexual assault are prohibited under the UCMJ, we interviewed service officials and male servicemembers at each location we visited who provided recent examples of such incidents occurring. For example, victim advocates and prosecutors at one installation described a series of escalating incidents that began with hitting the victim in the crotch, then throwing objects at the victim's crotch, and ultimately then saying the hazing would stop if the victim performed oral sex on the assailants. These service officials added that training on hazing-type activities and their relationship to sexual assault would be particularly beneficial to males in that it might lead to increased reporting and fewer inappropriate incidents. However, they stated that they have not seen this addressed in the training.

In our interviewer administered surveys with 122 male servicemembers during installation visits we asked a series of questions based on four scenarios that depicted graphic, initiation-type activities in an effort to gauge their level of awareness and acceptance of such incidents and that of their peers and supervisors.[89] While almost all survey participants found the situations the scenarios depicted to be unacceptable to some degree, at least 20 percent of participants of various ranks said they had heard of such activities occurring. Further, 6 of the 122 male servicemembers we surveyed volunteered first-hand accounts of witnessing a male servicemember being touched with the genitals of another male servicemember. Moreover, 2 of the 6 described their personal experiences; one mentioned being touched with the genitals of another male member at a military school and another mentioned both touching fellow servicemembers with his genitals and being touched with the genitals of other male servicemembers. Survey participants also told us that such incidents are largely unreported because it is just "locker room" behavior that men sometimes engage in when they are bored. In spite of the expectation that such activities would go unreported, in all but one scenario, at least half of the survey participants believed that their unit commander would be generally aware or aware of specific details if such a situation did occur. According to DOD officials, DOD has not more comprehensively addressed male sexual assault victims in its training materials because it has viewed its program as gender neutral, and it has focused the program mainly on female victims. However, a more thorough discussion in sexual assault training materials of how hazing and other behaviors may cross the line into sexual assault could increase awareness that such behaviors are not acceptable and help DOD transform its culture related to male sexual assault.

CONCLUSION

Sexual assaults of males have been overshadowed in both the military and civilian communities by the focus on female sexual assault victims. While sexual assaults of males are not unique to the military, DOD is in a unique position to lead on this issue, in that it has a program for sexual assault prevention and response for all its servicemembers, and the capability to collect and analyze data and develop responses targeted at male sexual assault victims. The U.S. military is overwhelmingly male, and while DOD has taken actions to address sexual assault of servicemembers generally, it had not until 2014 begun to take steps toward addressing sexual assault of male servicemembers specifically, despite initially identifying the need to focus on male victims as early as 2008. During the course of our review, DOD took preliminary steps including starting to develop implementation plans to increase male reporting of sexual assaults and collecting additional information about male sexual assault victims, that could help address the incidence of sexual assaults of males. However, DOD's lead office for sexual assault prevention and response had not used its full data collection on male sexual assault victims to inform program development in order to better target its future efforts, and had not established a plan for how its future program development will be informed by the data it collects. DOD's Office of the Assistant Secretary of Defense for Health Affairs also had not systematically evaluated the extent to which male victims have specific responses and needs following sexual assault or developed guidance for its providers department-wide, which could allow the military to better focus its programs in order to more fully meet the health-care needs of male victims.

Finally, elements of military culture can either aid or limit the prevention of, and responses to, sexual assaults of male servicemembers. According to key practices for organizational change, top leadership sets the tone and drives culture change. To date, DOD has not established goals and associated metrics related to male victims to help drive a transformation or culture change in DOD with regard to preventing sexual assaults of male servicemembers. Establishing such goals is key given the high level of turnover in DOD's SAPRO, which has had three different general officers in the director position since 2011. Moreover, there have been three Secretaries of Defense in the same period, further reducing continuity. Without clear goals and associated metrics to institutionalize efforts to address sexual assault of male servicemembers, such efforts will remain dependent on the individuals in office. Thus, developing such goals and metrics could give DOD a clear path forward and additional information to help it assess its progress in addressing sexual assault of males in the military and whether any changes are needed. While DOD has communicated to servicemembers about its sexual assault prevention efforts through means such as posters at installations, expanding these communications to depict male victims could further increase awareness of DOD's efforts specifically regarding sexual assaults of males. Hazing incidents can cross the line into sexual assault, but the department has not consistently included in its sexual assault training information on when hazing can also be sexual assault. The majority of the training to raise awareness in the military about sexual assault has not sufficiently depicted male victims. Expanding the training to include male victimization could better encourage male victim reporting and raise awareness and reduce stigmatization among commanders and servicemembers.

RECOMMENDATIONS FOR EXECUTIVE ACTION

To improve DOD's ability to prevent sexual assaults of male servicemembers and to increase its responsiveness to male servicemembers who are sexually assaulted, we are recommending that the Secretary of Defense take the following six actions:

- To help DOD's sexual assault prevention and response program realize the full benefit of the data it collects on sexual assault incidents, we recommend that the Secretary of Defense direct the Under Secretary of Defense for Personnel and Readiness, in collaboration with the Secretaries of the military services, to develop a plan for data-driven decision making to prioritize program efforts.
- To help ensure that all of DOD's medical and mental health providers are generally aware of any gender-specific needs of sexual assault victims, and that victims are provided the care that most effectively meets those needs, we are recommending that the Assistant Secretary of Defense for Health Affairs, in collaboration with the services' Surgeons General,
    - systematically evaluate the extent to which differences exist in the medical and mental health-care needs of male and female sexual assault victims, and the care regimen, if any, that will best meet those needs; and

- develop and issue guidance for the department's medical and mental health providers—and other personnel, as appropriate—based on the results of this evaluation that delineates these gender-specific distinctions and the care regimen that is recommended to most effectively meet those needs.
- To address challenges faced by male servicemembers as DOD continues to seek to transform its culture to address sexual assault, we are recommending that the Secretary of Defense direct the Under Secretary of Defense for Personnel and Readiness, in collaboration with the Secretaries of the military services, to
  - develop clear goals with associated metrics to drive the changes needed to address sexual assaults of males and articulate these goals, for example in the department's next sexual assault prevention strategy;
  - include information about the sexual victimization of males in communications to servicemembers that are used to raise awareness of sexual assault and the department's efforts to prevent and respond to it; and
  - revise sexual assault prevention and response training to more comprehensively and directly address the incidence of male servicemembers being sexually assaulted and how certain behavior and activities—like hazing—can constitute a sexual assault.

AGENCY COMMENTS AND OUR EVALUATION

We provided a draft of this report to DOD for review and comment. DOD concurred with each of our recommendations and also provided technical comments, which we incorporated in the report as appropriate.

In its written comments, DOD stated that it has already taken steps toward addressing three of our six recommendations.

- First, regarding our recommendation to develop a plan for data-driven decision making to prioritize program efforts, DOD concurred and noted that the department has taken steps over the past year to build a foundation of data sources to address male victimization as well as other aspects of sexual assault. DOD further noted recent steps that the department has begun to take related to male victims of sexual assault, such as military service efforts to develop a plan to improve male victim reporting, which we discuss in our report. We are encouraged by the department's efforts to improve its data on sexual assault and steps toward a greater focus on male sexual assault victims, and continue to believe that a plan for data-driven decision making would help to ensure such data is used to drive program decision making going forward.

- Second, with respect to our recommendation to systematically evaluate the extent to which differences exist in the medical and mental health-care needs of male and female sexual assault victims, and the care regimen, if any, that will best meet those needs, DOD concurred and noted that such efforts are already underway within the Army and will be forthcoming in the other services. While these are positive steps, we believe it is important for DOD and the military services to capitalize on the momentum of such initiatives and to ensure that it conducts a comprehensive evaluation of gender-specific aspects of victim care, especially including the mental health-care issues that were identified by and discussed with providers and subject-matter experts during our review and noted in our report.
- Third, with respect to our recommendation to develop and issue guidance for medical and mental health providers—and other personnel, as appropriate—based on the results of the evaluation that delineates gender-specific distinctions and the care regimen recommended to most effectively meet those needs, DOD concurred and noted that the Army and Navy have already begun such efforts and that other efforts are forthcoming in the other services. We are encouraged by the Army's efforts to further professionalize its sexual assault forensic examiners and want to underscore the importance of such steps being expanded to include the development of guidance that addresses both medical and mental health-care approaches for sexual assault victims and various types of providers, as is noted in our recommendation. Regarding the Navy's response that the Navy provides evidence-based care that is applicable regardless of the type of trauma or gender of victim being treated, we agree that there are universally applicable approaches to medical and mental health care; however, as we note in our report, specific guidance is key to help ensure that all providers—especially those who have never, but could potentially, treat a male victim of sexual assault—are generally aware

of any gender-specific approaches that can help maximize the effectiveness of care provided to victims of sexual assault.

Brenda S. Farrell
Director
Defense Capabilities and Management

APPENDIX I: SCOPE AND METHODOLOGY

To evaluate the extent to which the Department of Defense (DOD) has taken steps to prevent and respond to sexual assaults of male servicemembers, we reviewed DOD's and the military services' relevant guidance and requirements for the prevention of and response to sexual assault, as well as DOD reports and strategies on preventing and responding to sexual assault. In order to determine the successes of and challenges for prevention and response to sexual assault of male servicemembers, we visited four military installations in the United States and met with those who may have come into contact with male sexual assault victims, including sexual assault response coordinators; victim advocates; special victim counsels; chaplains; medical and mental health personnel; and commanders. We chose the four military installations we visited based on their high numbers of reported sexual assaults of male servicemembers relative to other installations within the same branch of service to maximize the possibility we would interview officials, responders, and care providers who had worked with male victims of sexual assault.[1] We also interviewed officials in the Under Secretary of Defense for Personnel and Readiness' Sexual Assault Prevention and Response Office (SAPRO), the Army, the Navy, the Marine Corps, and the Air Force to obtain a comprehensive understanding of their efforts to implement sexual assault and prevention programs. We compared DOD's rationale for how it prioritizes its sexual assault prevention and response efforts with leading practices for results-oriented management to determine the extent to which DOD uses the data it collects on sexual assault incidents to focus its efforts.[2]

In addition, at each of the installations we visited, we obtained male servicemembers' perspectives on DOD's prevention and response to sexual assault program by conducting interviewer-administered surveys with male servicemembers.[3] Specifically, at these visits, we collectively surveyed 122 randomly selected male servicemembers of various ranks through interviewer administered surveys with a scenario-based component (see app. II for the interview questions and scenarios). To select servicemembers for participation in the survey, we requested lists of male servicemembers in selected units from each installation in advance of visiting the installation. To the extent possible, we requested that these lists not include servicemembers who were not available to participate in our survey. We then organized the servicemembers into four rank categories—junior enlisted, junior officer, senior enlisted, and senior officer—and assigned a randomized number to each servicemember. Participants were categorized according to the following ranks: junior enlisted (encompassing the ranks of E1–E4); senior enlisted (encompassing the ranks of E5–E7); junior officers (encompassing the ranks of O1–O3); and senior officers (encompassing the ranks of O4– O5). We listed the servicemembers by category and assigned number in ascending order, provided the lists to installation officials for them to schedule the servicemember participant surveys, beginning with the servicemembers at the top of the list, until spots were filled for the rank category. Because we did not select participants using a statistically representative sampling method, the information provided from the surveys is nongeneralizable and therefore cannot be projected across DOD, a service, or any single installation we visited. However, the survey results and comments provide insight into the command climate at the time of our visit. Table 1 shows the installations we visited and the number of male servicemembers we interviewed by rank.

Table 1. Number of Surveys Administered by Location

Installation	Junior enlisted	Senior enlisted	Junior officer	Senior officer	Total
Marine Corps Base Camp Pendleton, Camp Pendleton, California	14	5	11	4	34
Keesler Air Force Base, Biloxi, Mississippi	12	4	13	4	33
Fort Bliss Army Base, El Paso, Texas	6	1	6	4	17
Norfolk Naval Base, Norfolk, Virginia	12	5	16	5	38
Total	44	15	46	17	122

Source: GAO. | GAO-15-284

To develop our survey questions, we interviewed outside experts, including two individual experts and experts at one institution, identified through our prior work in the area of sexual assault in the military, as well as advocacy groups for male servicemember sexual assault victims and reviewed our prior work related to DOD's sexual assault prevention and response program. We also reviewed research related to sexual assault and male victims. We worked with social science survey specialists to develop our survey questionnaires. The four scenarios within the survey were based on male-on-male activities that we learned of in our research that differ from penetrative sexual acts and that might be considered sexual assault, depending on the particular circumstances. Because these were not sample surveys, there are no sampling errors. However, the practical difficulties of conducting any survey may introduce errors, commonly referred to as nonsampling errors. For example, differences in how a particular question is interpreted, the sources of information that are available to respondents, or how data are entered into a database can introduce unwanted variability into the survey results. We took steps in the development of the questionnaires, the data collection, and the data analysis to minimize these nonsampling errors. For example, prior to administering the survey, we pretested the content and format of the questionnaire with male analysts at GAO with military experience who were not involved in this project to determine whether (1) the survey questions were clear, (2) the terms used were precise, (3) respondents were able to provide the information we were seeking, and (4) the questions were unbiased. We made changes to the content and format of our final questionnaire based on the results of our pretesting. Finally, each team member was trained in the administration of the interviewer-administered survey to assure its consistent implementation across installations and selected participants.

Because of the sensitivity of the information being presented and discussed in the survey, we took several steps to help ensure a confidential and safe environment during the interviewer-administered sessions. First, we consulted with mental health professionals to be prepared with resources if we encountered servicemembers who had experienced sexual assault. In the survey administration, we did not document the names of participants and we conducted the surveys one-on-one in private offices or meeting rooms that were apart from main lobby or gathering areas. During the scenario-based portion of the survey, we handed the service member each scenario printed on a card, one at a time, allowing the participant time to read and react to the scenario at his own pace before the interviewer asked a series of follow-up questions. This was repeated for each of the four scenarios.

In order to obtain the perspectives of male servicemember sexual assault victims, we interviewed current and former male servicemember victims of sexual assault who volunteered to speak with us about their perspectives on the military and its response to sexual assaults.[4] We developed the interview protocol for male servicemember sexual assault victims using a similar process as the survey of selected male servicemembers. Rather than pretest the instrument with victims of sexual assault, we consulted with mental health professionals on the appropriateness of the instrument as well as guidance on resources to offer participants if relevant.

We obtained and analyzed data on reported incidents of sexual assault contained in DOD's annual reports on sexual assault to Congress for fiscal years 2008 through 2013 and fiscal year 2014 data provided by SAPRO.[5] Through fiscal year 2013 SAPRO did not collect information on the victim gender for restricted reports converting to unrestricted; therefore, we calculated the minimum number of reports by male and female victims, respectively, that could have remained unconverted. This provided us the minimum number of servicemembers of each gender that would be included in the unconverted restricted reports. We classified the remaining unconverted restricted reports as of unknown victim gender since the gender of the victim for those reports could not be precisely determined. We also determined that the data on reports of sexual assault in DOD's annual reports were sufficiently reliable for the purposes for which we use them in this report. We assessed the reliability of DOD's data on the number of reported victims of sexual assault by gender by (1) performing electronic testing for obvious errors in accuracy and completeness, (2) reviewing existing information about the data and the systems that produced them, and (3) interviewing agency officials knowledgeable about the data. Due to the confidential nature of the collection of restricted reports, there are some limitations to fully assessing the reliability of the number and gender of servicemember victims in restricted reports. However, despite these limitations, we determined that DOD's annual reports for fiscal years 2008 through 2013 and the fiscal year 2014 data provided by SAPRO were sufficiently reliable for use in determining the reported number of servicemember victims of sexual assault by gender. We also reviewed DOD's prevalence studies, which include estimates[6] of servicemembers subjected to unwanted sexual contact or sexual assault in fiscal years 2010, 2012, and 2014.[7]

To evaluate the extent to which DOD's sexual assault prevention and response program is meeting the medical and mental health-care needs of male victims of sexual assault, we obtained and analyzed DOD's and the military services' relevant policies and guidance establishing medical and mental health-care requirements for the response to sexual assault. We also interviewed officials in DOD, the Army, the Navy, the Marine Corps, and the Air Force to obtain an understanding of their efforts to meet the medical and mental health-care needs of male victims of sexual assault. Further, we met with program officials, sexual assault response coordinators, victim advocates, and medical and mental health-care providers at each of the four installations we visited. In order to obtain perspectives from male sexual assault victims, we interviewed current and former male servicemember victims of sexual assault who volunteered to speak with us about their perspectives on the military's mental health and medical services following sexual assault. We also interviewed outside experts and healthcare providers with experience working with male sexual assault victims, as well as advocacy groups for male servicemember sexual assault victims.[8]

We also compared DOD's latest guidance from 2013 on providing gender-responsive care to sexual assault victims with leading practices for program evaluation to determine the extent to which DOD has systematically evaluated program needs.[9] We conducted a literature review of academic and research articles published from January 2008 through September 2014[10] that addressed male victims' responses to sexual assault and about male sexual assault victims in order to identify and summarize findings and existing research on gender differences in sexual assault responses as well as on male victim needs. For our literature review, we searched the BIOSIS Previews; British Library Inside Conferences; EMBASE; EMCare; MEDLINE; NTIS: National Technical Information Service; Public Affairs Information Service International; PsycINFO; and ProQuest databases using search terms, including words relating to males (e.g., "male," "males," "men," and "man"), words relating to sexual assault victims (e.g., "victim" and "survivor"), and words related to sexual assault (e.g., "sexual assault" and "rape"). We excluded those that only discussed female victims of sexual assault, child-abuse victims, as well as any that did not discuss male sexual assault victims or victim responses and needs following sexual assault. We found a total of 36 articles and publications that met our inclusion criteria. We did not independently evaluate the validity of the articles' findings.

To evaluate the extent to which the culture of the U.S. military poses distinct challenges for preventing and responding to sexual assault of male servicemembers, we interviewed officials with DOD's and the military services' respective sexual assault prevention and response offices to obtain an understanding of challenges officials encounter in preventing and responding to sexual assault of male servicemembers. To assess primary communications used by DOD and the services on sexual assault, we reviewed posters used by

DOD and each service to raise awareness among servicemembers about DOD's sexual assault prevention and response efforts and to convey departmental values regarding sexual assault. We selected those posters available on the SAPRO's website that were available at the time we conducted this review, those used during 2007 through 2014.[11] We obtained sexual assault training material from these offices and reviewed them for scenarios involving male victims, scenarios involving hazing, and slides directly applicable to leadership and command-climate issues. Further, at each of the four installations we visited, we met with sexual assault response coordinators; victim advocates; legal officials including special victim counsels and victim legal counsels; chaplains; medical and mental health personnel; and commanders in order to gain their perspective on distinct challenges for preventing and responding to sexual assault of male servicemembers. In addition, at each of the installations we visited, we obtained male servicemembers' perspectives on DOD's prevention and response program by conducting interviewer administered surveys with male servicemembers.

Additionally, we spoke with officials at the Defense Equal Opportunity Management Institute to understand the command-climate survey process and the sexual assault prevention and response portions of the survey. We obtained examples of the administered surveys and reviewed them to understand the questions posed and how results are delivered to commanders. We used our interviews with male victims to gather additional information on the military culture surrounding incidents of, and responses to, sexual assault. We also reviewed relevant reports and studies on the subject of sexual assault in the military. We also interviewed outside experts with experience working with male sexual assault victims as well as advocacy groups for male servicemember sexual assault victims, as discussed above. Finally, we compared steps DOD has taken on sexual assault prevention and response with leading practices for organizational change to determine what, if any, steps DOD could take to foster an environment in which male servicemembers are more likely to report that they have been sexually assaulted.[12]

Tables 2 and 3 present the DOD and non-DOD organizations we met with during our review.

Table 2. DOD Locations Visited or Contacted

Organization	Location visited or contacted
Department of Defense	•Sexual AssaultPrevention and Response Office (SAPRO), Alexandria, Virginia
Department of the Army	•Sexual Harassment / Assault Response and Prevention Program, Arlington, Virginia •U. S. Army Medical Command •Fort Bliss Army Base, El Paso, Texas
Department of the Navy	•Sexual Assault Prevention and Response Office, Arlington, Virginia •Bureau of Medicine and Surgery, Falls Church, Virginia
United States Navy	•Sexual Assault Prevention and Response Office, Arlington, Virginia •Office of Hazing Prevention, Arlington, Virginia •Norfolk Naval Base, Norfolk, Virginia
United States Marine Corps	•Sexual Assault Prevention and Response Office, Quantico, Virginia •Marine Corps Base Camp Pendleton, Camp Pendleton, California
Department of the Air Force	•Sexual Assault Prevention and Response Office, Arlington, Virginia •Air Force Medical Service •Keesler Air Force Base, Biloxi, Mississippi

Source: GAO. | GAO-15-284

Table 3. Non-DOD Organizations and Individuals Visited or Contacted

Category	Organization or Individual visited or contacted
Department of Veterans Affairs	•Veterans Health Administration, Washington, D.C. •Bay Pines VA Healthcare System, Bay Pines, Florida
Nongovernmental organizations	•RAND Corporation •Protect Our Defenders, Washington, D.C. •Gulf Coast Women's Center For Nonviolence; Mississippi •University Behavioral Health of El Paso, El Paso, Texas •Sentara Norfolk General Hospital, Norfolk, Virginia

Category	Organization or Individual visited or contacted
	•Chesapeake Forensic Specialist, Chesapeake, Virginia
Subject-matter experts	•Dr. Rebecca Hannagan, Associate Professor, Center for the Study of Family Violence andSexual Abuse, Northern Illinois University •Dr. David Lisak

Source: GAO. | GAO-15-284.

We conducted this performance audit from November 2013 to March 2015 in accordance with generally accepted government auditing standards. Those standards require that we plan and perform the audit to obtain sufficient, appropriate evidence to provide a reasonable basis for our findings and conclusions based on our audit objectives. We believe that the evidence obtained provides a reasonable basis for our findings and conclusions based on our audit objectives.

Appendix II: Interviewer-Administered Survey of Male Servicemembers

To obtain servicemembers' perspectives on issues regarding sexual assault prevention and response programs in the Department of Defense (DOD), we selected four installations to visit while ensuring each military service was represented. At these site visits, we collectively met with and surveyed 122 randomly selected male servicemembers of various ranks through interviewer-administered surveys with a scenario-based component (see app. I for the full scope and methodology for the survey). We organized the servicemembers into four rank categories—junior enlisted, junior officer, senior enlisted, and senior officer.[1] Because we did not select participants using a statistically representative sampling method, the perspectives obtained during our interview sessions are nongeneralizable and therefore cannot be projected across DOD, an individual branch of service, or any single installation we visited.

Below are the questions from the survey and a summary of the results in tables 4 through 13.

Survey Questions for Male Servicemembers

Good morning/afternoon. My name is ______ and I am with the U.S. Government Accountability Office, or GAO.

GAO is an independent, nonpartisan agency that conducts research on a variety of issues that are of interest to Congress. For our particular review, we are studying types of experiences that servicemembers may have in their units. In our review, we will have the opportunity to talk to program officials, installation leadership, and other groups. However, we feel it is very valuable to talk with individual servicemembers as well. We will not in any way identify you either in our report or to anyone in the military. All of the information we discuss today will be completely confidential.

First, I would like to ask some information about you. None of this information will be used to identify you but is information that will help to provide us with context for our survey.

1. How long have you been in the military?

Table 4. Respondents' Length of Time in the Military by Rank Group

Response	Junior enlisted	Senior enlisted	Junior officer	Senior officer	Total numberof respondents
less than 1 year	2	0	2	0	4
between 1 to less than 6 years	42	5	19	0	66
between 6 to less than 11 years	0	2	16	0	18
between 11 to less than 21 years	0	6	9	14	29
21 years or over	0	2	0	3	5
Total number of respondents	44	15	46	17	122

Source: GAO. | GAO-15-284

2. What is your rank?

Table 5. Respondents' Military Rank Group

	Number of respondents
Junior enlisted	**44**
Senior enlisted	**15**
Junior officer	**46**
Senior officer	**17**
Total number of respondents	**122**

Source: GAO. | GAO-15-284

3. How long have you been with your unit of assignment?

Table 6. Respondents' Length of Time Assigned to Current Unit by Rank Group

Response	Junior enlisted	Senior enlisted	Junior officer	Senior officer	Total numberof respondents
less than 1 year	15	3	22	6	46
between 1 to less than 3 years	20	7	20	8	55
between 3 to less than 5 years	7	5	4	2	18
between 5 to less than 7 years	2	0	0	0	2
7 years or over	0	0	0	1	1
Total number of respondents	44	15	46	17	122

Source: GAO. | GAO-15-284

4. Do you have both men and women in your unit of assignment?

Yes □
No □
Don't know □

Table 7. Extent to Which Respondents' Unit Have both Men and Women Assigned, by Rank Group

Response	Junior enlisted	Senior enlisted	Junior officer	Senior officer	Total number ofrespondents
Yes	36	14	43	17	110
No	7	1	3	0	11
Did not answer	1	0	0	0	1
Total number of respondents	44	15	46	17	122

Source: GAO. | GAO-15-284

Next, I would like to ask you some questions about your unit.

5. Based on your experience in the service, what pranks or rites of passage occur when servicemembers are hanging out off-duty?

6. We've heard about a variety of "pranks" or "horsing around" that servicemembers may encounter. Sometimes these may occur, for example when a servicemember joins the military or when he or she joins a new unit. Some of these pranks or horsing around activities are of a sensitive nature. We have cards which describe situations we've identified as part of our review that have occurred among servicemembers. We'll start with situation A (and separately, B, C, and D). After you read through the card we can discuss whether you've heard of this type of thing occurring.

Below describe the situations presented to the survey participants on cards.

Table 8. Situations Presented to Respondent on Separate Cards for Question 6 of Survey

Situation	Situation description
A	Serviceman Jones recently transferred to a new unit. When he arrives, several members from his new unit volunteer to show him around and to fill him in on how the unit operates. Towards the end of his "introduction" to the unit, one member of the unit jokingly mentions that Jones won't "officially" be part of the unit until he administers a "credit card swipe" to someone of equal rank, which the member of the unit demonstrates by pretending to "swipe" his hand between the buttocks.

Situation	Situation description
B	Soon after lights out, Serviceman Taylor gets up to use the restroom. When he returns to his bunk, he pulls back the covers and finds Serviceman Barnes laying there completely naked. Serviceman Barnes says "Gotcha" and all the other men in the quarters share a laugh.
C	Serviceman Smith, who recently arrived at a new unit, is sleeping in his rack late one night. He is startled awake by a group of guys from his new unit. When he rolls over to see what happened, one of the guys slaps Smith on the forehead with his genitals. The group laughs, and several exclaim "welcome" as the group breaks up.
D	While at a BBQ with other members of his unit, Serviceman Sanchez drank too much and was taken back to the barracks to "sleep it off." Several hours later, other members of the unit returned to the barracks drunk and thought it would be funnyto play some practical jokes on Serviceman Sanchez since he was sleeping. For the grand finale, Seaman Jones "teabagged" Sanchez by putting his scrotum on Sanchez's face.

Source: GAO. | GAO-15-284

Questions 6a through 6d were asked separately for each situation after the survey participant read the printed card. For example, after the participant read the card describing Situation A, the interviewer asked each question, 6a–6d, in sequence. This was repeated for Situations B, C, and D.

6a. For situation __, have you heard of this type of thing occurring?

Yes □
No □
Don't know □

Table 9. Extent to Which Respondents Have Heard of Situations A, B, C, and D Occurring, by Rank Group

Situation	Response	Junior enlisted	Senior enlisted	Junior officer	Senior officer	Total number of respondents
A	Yes	12	4	11	3	30
	No	32	11	35	14	92
	Don't know	0	0	0	0	0
	Did not answer	0	0	0	0	0

Table 9. (Continued)

Situation	Response	Junior enlisted	Senior enlisted	Junior officer	Senior officer	Total number of respondents
	Total number of respondents	44	15	46	17	122
B	Yes	8	6	9	1	24
	No	36	8	37	15	96
	Don't know	0	0	0	0	0
	Did not answer	0	1	0	1	2
	Total number of respondents	44	15	46	17	122
C	Yes	11	6	5	5	27
	No	33	9	41	12	95
	Don't know	0	0	0	0	0
	Did not answer	0	0	0	0	0
	Total number of respondents	44	15	46	17	122
D	Yes	16	10	16	6	48
	No	28	3	29	11	71
	Don't know	0	0	0	0	0
	Did not answer	0	2	1	0	3
	Total number of respondents	44	15	46	17	122

Source: GAO. | GAO-15-284

6b. In general, how acceptable or unacceptable do you think this type of situation would be for other members of your unit?

6c. Would you say that something like situation _ occurs: never, rarely, occasionally, sometimes, or often?

Never □
Rarely □
Occasionally □

Sometimes ☐
Often ☐

Table 10. Respondents' Views on Extent to Which Situations A, B, C, and D Occur by Rank Group

Situation	Response	Junior enlisted	Senior enlisted	Junior officer	Senior officer	Total number of responses
A	Never	19	3	12	8	42
	Rarely	14	4	20	5	43
	Occasionally	6	3	5	2	16
	Sometimes	3	4	5	0	12
	Often	0	0	0	1	1
	Did not answer	2	2	5	1	10
	Total	44	16	47	17	124
B	Never	18	2	14	8	42
	Rarely	15	9	23	7	54
	Occasionally	8	1	8	0	17
	Sometimes	3	2	2	1	8
	Often	0	0	0	0	0
	Did not answer	0	2	2	1	5
	Grand Total	44	16	49	17	126
C	Never	20	3	19	10	52
	Rarely	15	8	21	6	50
	Occasionally	4	2	3	2	11
	Sometimes	4	1	2	0	7
	Often	0	0	1	0	1
	Did not answer	2	1	3	1	7
	Grand Total	45	15	49	19	128
D	Never	17	1	13	8	39
	Rarely	13	4	19	7	43
	Occasionally	7	4	10	0	21
	Sometimes	4	2	2	1	9
	Often	1	1	1	1	4
	Did not answer	3	3	2	0	8
	Grand Total	45	15	47	17	124

Source: GAO. | GAO-15-284

Note: Responses do not add up to 122 because some respondents provided multiple answers.

6d. Would you say that unit leadership would be generally aware, aware of specific details or not at all aware of something like situation _? (Check all that apply)

Generally aware ☐
Aware of specific details ☐
Not at all aware ☐
Don't know ☐

Table 11. Respondents' Views on Extent to Which Unit Leadership Would Be Aware of Situations A, B, C, and D Occurring by Rank Group

Situation	Response	Junior enlisted	Senior enlisted	Junior officer	Senior officer	Total number of responses
A	Generally aware	19	5	21	4	49
	Aware of specific details	11	1	4	3	19
	Not at all aware	12	7	14	7	40
	Don't know	0	1	0	1	2
	Did not answer	8	2	9	3	22
	Total	50	16	48	18	132
B	Generally aware	11	2	10	3	26
	Aware of specific details	11	3	7	4	25
	Not at all aware	18	8	22	6	54
	Don't know	1	0	1	1	3
	Did not answer	6	2	8	4	20
	Total	47	15	48	18	128
C	Generally aware	13	5	9	3	30
	Aware of specific details	15	3	13	4	35

Situation	Response	Junior enlisted	Senior enlisted	Junior officer	Senior officer	Total number of responses
	Not at all aware	14	7	19	5	45
	Don't know	1	0	1	2	4
	Did not answer	4	1	6	3	14
	Total	47	16	48	17	128
D	Generally aware	15	5	16	4	40
	Aware of specific details	17	2	11	6	36
	Not at all aware	14	5	16	4	39
	Don't know	0	0	1	1	2
	Did not answer	3	3	3	2	11
	Total	49	15	47	17	128

Source: GAO. | GAO-15-284

Note: Responses do not add up to 122 because some respondents provided multiple answers.

Thank you for talking through these situations with us. We know these topics are very sensitive. We have a few more questions before we wrap things up.

7. We have presented several scenarios describing acts that are unwanted and sexual in nature. If you experienced any kind of unwanted sexual contact, would you have any reservations about reporting it?

Yes	□	Go to question 7b
No	□	Skip to question 8
Don't know	□	Skip to question 8

Table 12. Respondents' Views on Whether They Would Have Reservations about Reporting Any Kind of Unwanted Sexual Contact, by Rank Group

Response	Junior enlisted	Senior enlisted	Junior officer	Senior officer	Total number of respondents
Yes	6	1	8	2	17
No	34	9	34	15	92
Don't know	1	1	2	0	4
Did not answer	3	4	2	0	9
Total number of respondents	44	15	46	17	122

Source: GAO. | GAO-15-284

7b. Could you describe for us the reservations?

8. Do you think other servicemembers may have reservations about reporting an instance of unwanted sexual contact?

Yes	□	Go to question 8b
No	□	Skip to question 9
Don't know	□	Skip to question 9

Table 13. Respondents' Views on Whether They Believe Others Would Have Reservations about Reporting Any Kind of Unwanted Sexual Contact, by Rank Group

Response	Junior enlisted	Senior enlisted	Junior officer	Senior officer	Total number of respondents
Yes	32	13	31	11	87
No	6	1	9	6	22
Don't know	2	1	0	0	3
Did not answer	4	0	6	0	10
Total number of respondents	44	15	46	17	122

Source: GAO. | GAO-15-284

8b. Could you talk to us about some of the reservations that servicemembers may have to report such incidents? And, whether you think that it is likely that those reservations would cause a servicemember not to report the incident?

9. What, if anything do male servicemembers want from their command to address sexual harassment and/or sexual assault incidents? We are particularly interested in hearing about anything that may be particular to male servicemembers.

10. Do you have any other thoughts or concerns you would like to share concerning the topics we've covered?

Thank you for taking the time to participate in this survey. As I mentioned at the beginning, we will treat all of your comments anonymously. There is no attribution to you for the specific comments you made today. Our goal is to provide the best data possible and you have helped us greatly today with your comments and insights.

Thank you again for your participation.

Appendix III: Questionnaire for Interviews with Male Servicemember Sexual Assault Victims

In order to obtain the perspectives of male servicemember sexual assault victims, we interviewed current and former male servicemember victims of sexual assault who volunteered to speak with us about their perspectives on the military and its response to sexual assaults. We announced GAO's interest in anonymously interviewing male servicemembers who experienced sexual assault and provided a toll-free telephone number and email address for volunteers to contact us. Officials in DOD's Sexual Assault Prevention and Response Office, the department's lead office for sexual assault prevention and response, volunteered to post our announcement on the DOD Safe Helpline website, and we also disseminated the announcement through program and installation officials, advocacy groups, and subject matter experts. Further details about our methodology for these interviews can be found in appendix I. The survey follows.

1. Are you calling about an assault that you experienced or are you calling about an assault experienced by someone else?

My experience	□	Go to next question
Someone else's experience	□	Go to separate interview

I. Demographic/Background Information

1. Did the assault occur while serving in the military?	O Yes ________________ (document branch of service and continue to next question)
	O No (end discussion-see script)
	O Don't Know (end discussion-see script)
	O Prefer not to answer (end discussion-see script)
2. What was your rank at the time of the assault?	___________________________________
3. What year did the assault occur?	_______________
4. Did you know the person who assaulted you?	O Yes
	O No
	O Don't Know
	O Prefer not to answer
5. Was the person who assaulted you another	O Yes
	O No
servicemember?	O Don't Know
	O Prefer not to answer

II. Reporting

6. Did you report the assault? a. If yes, what year was the assault reported? b. To whom was the assault reported?	O Yes O No ______________ ____________________________________
7. How did you decide whether or not to report the assault? Based on the caller's response, follow up to ensure that we get clarification on the following items: a. Was your decision to report related to your service in the military? If so, how? b. Was your decision to report related to your gender? If so, how?	____________________________________ ____________________________________ ____________________________________ ____________________________________ ____________________________________ ____________________________________
8. Based on your experience, would you change your decision about reporting the assault? How would you do things differently?	O Yes O No O Don't know ____________________________________ ____________________________________
9. We understand that more male servicemembers experience victimization than report it. In your opinion, what could DOD do to increase the number of male servicemembers who report that they were sexually assaulted?	____________________________________ ____________________________________ ____________________________________
10. What, if any, advice would you give a male servicemember who is trying to decide whether to report that he was sexually assaulted?	____________________________________ ____________________________________ ____________________________________ ____________________________________

III. Response to Assault

11. Did you receive any services related to the assault? ***If the caller did not receive services, skip to question #16.	O Yes O No O Don't Know
12. What type of services were you offered? What type of services did you receive? Based on the caller's response, follow up to ensure that we get clarification on the following items: a. Were any of the services offered/provided male-specific? b. In your opinion, are there male-specific services that DOD should provide?	____________________ ____________________ ____________________ ____________________ ____________________ ____________________ ____________________
13. Were there services that you would have liked to have been available but were not? a. Did the services that DOD did provide following the assault meet your needs as a male? Please explain.	O Yes O No O Somewhat O Don't know ____________________ ____________________

14. What, if anything would you recommend that the [insert service] do to be more responsive to male servicemembers who are sexually assaulted?	______ ______ ______
IV. Miscellaneous 15. To what extent did the recently repealed policy of "Don't Ask, Don't Tell" (DADT) have on your willingness to report?	______ ______ ______ ______
16. Is there anything, other than what we have already discussed, that you would recommend DOD do to encourage more male victims to report that they were sexually assaulted? a. Anything related to male victims of sexual assault that we didn't discuss but you think we should be aware of?	______ ______ ______ ______ ______

End Notes

[1] Federal Bureau of Investigation, Frequently Asked Questions about the Change in the Definition of Rape (May 20, 2013).

[2] DOD, Department of Defense Annual Report on Sexual Assault in the Military, Fiscal Year 2013 (Apr. 22, 2014), Department of Defense Annual Report on Sexual Assault in the Military, Fiscal Year 2012 (May 3, 2013), Department of Defense Annual Report on Sexual Assault in the Military, Fiscal Year 2011 (Apr. 12, 2012), Department of Defense Annual Report on Sexual Assault in the Military, Fiscal Year 2010 (March 2011), Department of Defense Fiscal Year 2009 Annual Report on Sexual Assault in the Military (March 2010), Department of Defense FY08 Report on Sexual Assault in the Military (Mar. 12, 2009), and fiscal year 2014 data provided on Mar. 2, 2015, by DOD's Sexual Assault Prevention and Response Office (SAPRO).

[3] RAND Corporation, Sexual Assault and Sexual Harassment in the Military: Top-Line Estimates for Active-Duty Service Members from the 2014 RAND Military Workplace Study, Annex 1 to Department of Defense, Report to the President of the United States on Sexual Assault Prevention and Response (Nov. 25, 2014).

[4] See Ronald W. Reagan National Defense Authorization Act for Fiscal Year 2005, Pub. L. No. 108-375, §577 (2004).

[5] We also made recommendations to the Coast Guard. See GAO, Military Personnel: DOD's and the Coast Guard's Sexual Assault Prevention and Response Programs Face Implementation and Oversight Challenges, GAO-08-924 (Washington, D.C.: Aug. 29, 2008). DOD and the Coast Guard concurred with all of our recommendations.

[6] Specifically, we recommended that DOD take 10 actions, including identifying how the results of performance assessments would be used to guide the development of future program initiatives, identifying how the Office of the Secretary of Defense's program resources correlate to its achievement of strategic program objectives, and standardizing the type, amount, and format of the data in the military services' annual reports on sexual assault, See GAO, Military Personnel: Additional Actions Are Needed to Strengthen DOD's and the Coast Guard's Sexual Assault Prevention and Response Programs, GAO-10-215 (Washington, D.C.: Feb. 3, 2010).

[7] GAO, Military Personnel: DOD Has Taken Steps to Meet the Health Needs of Deployed Servicewomen, but Actions Are Needed to Enhance Care for Sexual Assault Victims, GAO-13-182 (Washington, D.C.: Jan. 29, 2013).

[8] DOD stated that it did not concur with this recommendation, and provided examples of steps it had taken that might help to address the report's findings, such as revising its instruction on the sexual assault prevention and response program to address health-care provider procedures and health-care providers' responsibilities related to sexual assault forensic-examination kits.

[9] See H.R. Rep. No. 113-102 (2013) accompanying H.R. 1960, a proposed bill for the National Defense Authorization Act for Fiscal Year 2014.

[10] H.R. Rep. No. 113-102 (2013).

[11] We did not use data prior to fiscal year 2008 because DOD did not report on the victim gender of all unrestricted sexual assault reports involving servicemember victims until fiscal year 2008. Fiscal year 2014 was the most recent complete year of data available.

[12] DOD reports these estimates with a 95 percent confidence interval. We used the confidence intervals to calculate the likely ranges of the number of DOD servicemembers in order to reflect the uncertainty surrounding the estimates.

[13] DOD typically conducts its Workplace and Gender Relations Surveys of active-duty servicemembers every 2 years to obtain the data used to calculate these estimates. In 2014, for similar purposes, RAND Corporation conducted the 2014 Military Workplace Study on behalf of DOD. The last three surveys were conducted for fiscal years 2010, 2012, and 2014. Prior to that, the last survey conducted was in 2006. For the purpose of our analysis, we only included reporting data and estimates of unwanted sexual contact or sexual assault back to 2008 since, according to SAPRO officials, data on reported sexual assaults prior to 2008 were not as reliable.

[14] The four military installations we visited were chosen based on their high numbers of reported sexual assaults of male servicemembers relative to other installations within the same branch of service in order to maximize the possibility we would interview officials, responders, and care providers who had worked with male victims of sexual assault. While the information obtained at these four installations is not generalizable across DOD or any

military service, it enabled us to obtain the perspectives of commanders, servicemembers, and officials who provide services to sexual assault victims.

15 Survey participants were selected randomly to reflect a range of ranks within four rank categories at the installations we visited; however, the comments provided by servicemembers are nongeneralizable and therefore cannot be projected across DOD, a service, or any single installation. The interviewer-administered surveys involved a GAO analyst interviewing a male servicemember using a predetermined set of questions and recording the servicemember's responses.

16 As of December 2014, we interviewed 12 male victims who voluntarily contacted us to discuss being sexually assaulted while serving in the U.S. military. While all the male victims had served in and experienced one or more sexual assaults while serving in the U.S. military, some were not servicemembers currently. To solicit voluntary participation, we announced GAO's interest in anonymously interviewing male servicemembers who experienced sexual assault and provided a toll-free telephone number and email address for volunteers to contact us. SAPRO offered and posted our announcement on the DOD Safe Helpline website, and we also disseminated the announcement through program and installation officials, advocacy groups, and subject-matter experts. Our interviews of male victims of sexual assault in the military are not generalizable across any population, but enabled us to obtain the perspectives of those who had directly experienced a sexual assault while serving in the military, including their experience, in some cases, of reporting the assault and seeking care.

17 GAO, Managing for Results: Enhancing Agency Use of Performance Information for Management Decision Making, GAO-05-927 (Washington, D.C.: Sept. 9, 2005). To identify these leading practices, we reviewed relevant literature including previous GAO reports, spoke with experts in using performance information, and held group discussions with federal program managers. We also interviewed individuals from five federal agencies and reviewed documentation to illustrate how program managers have used performance information to make decisions. We identified uses for performance information including identifying problems and taking action, developing strategy and allocating resources, recognizing and rewarding performance, and identifying and sharing effective approaches. See GAO-05-927 for additional details on the scope and methodology for identifying these leading practices.

18 GAO, Program Evaluation: Studies Helped Agencies Measure or Explain Program Performance, GAO/GGD-00-204 (Washington, D.C.: Sept. 29, 2000). To identify these leading practices, we conducted case studies of how some agencies have already used evaluation studies and methods in their performance reports. Based on the cases we reviewed, we identified that evaluations were generally used to develop or improve upon agencies' measures of program performance or to better understand performance and how it might be improved. See GAO/GGD-00-204 for additional details on the scope and methodology for identifying these leading practices.

19 We reviewed the following GAO reports related to creating results-oriented cultures and effecting organization change: GAO, Human Capital: A Guide for Assessing Strategic Training and Development Efforts in the Federal Government, GAO-04-546G (Washington, D.C.: Mar. 1, 2004). For that report, GAO obtained information through consultations with government officials and experts in the private sector, academia, and nonprofit organizations; examination of laws and regulations related to training and development in the federal government; and reviewing the body of literature on training and development issues, including prior GAO reports. GAO, Results-Oriented Cultures:

Implementation Steps to Assist Mergers and Organizational Transformations, GAO-03-669 (Washington, D.C.: July 2, 2003). For that report, we convened a forum to identify useful practices and lessons learned from major private- and public-sector organizational mergers, acquisitions, and transformations. GAO, Mergers and Transformation: Lessons Learned for a Department of Homeland Security and Other Federal Agencies, GAO-03-293SP (Washington, D.C.: Nov. 14, 2002). For that report, we convened a forum to identify useful practices from major private- and public-sector organizational mergers, acquisitions, and transformations. GAO, Organizational Culture: Techniques Companies Use to Perpetuate or Change Beliefs or Values, GAO/NSIAD-92-105 (Washington, D.C.: Feb. 27, 1992). For that report, we obtained the views of private-sector experts on techniques used to change or perpetuate an organizational culture.

[20] Department of Defense Directive 6495.01, Sexual Assault Prevention and Response (SAPR) Program (Jan. 23, 2012). (Incorporating Change 1, Apr. 30, 2013). (Hereinafter cited as DOD Directive 6495.01.)

[21] DOD Directive 6495.01.

[22] Department of Defense, Secretary of Defense Memorandum, Withholding Initial Disposition Authority Under the Uniform Code of Military Justice in Certain Sexual Assault Cases (Apr. 20, 2012).

[23] DOD Directive 6495.01. DOD's annual reports to Congress on sexual assaults also include cadets and midshipmen at the military service academies.

[24] Department of Defense Directive 5136.01, Assistant Secretary of Defense for Health Affairs, (ASD(HA)) (Sept. 30, 2013).

[25] In contrast to the other services, the Army's program that is responsible for dealing with sexual assaults also deals with sexual harassment. The Army's program is called the Sexual Harassment/Assault Response and Prevention (SHARP) program whereas the other programs are referred to as Sexual Assault Prevention and Response (SAPR).

[26] DOD Directive 6495.01.

[27] Department of Defense Instruction 6495.02, Sexual Assault Prevention and Response (SAPR) Program Procedures (Mar. 28, 2013) (incorporating Change 1, Feb. 12, 2014), encl. 5. (Hereinafter cited as DOD Instruction 6495.02.)

[28] As noted previously, these male sexual assault victims were not necessarily in military service at the time we spoke with them.

[29] SAPRO officials noted that there is no requirement in DOD policy or military law for a sexual assault to be reported to a servicemember's chain of command. Sexual assault reports may be made to a variety of officials, including sexual assault response coordinators, victim advocates, law-enforcement personnel, and criminal investigators.

[30] The 122 randomly selected male servicemembers were separately asked during our interviewer-administered surveys (1) if they experienced any kind of unwanted sexual contact, would they have any reservations about reporting it and (2) whether they think other servicemembers may have reservations about reporting an instance of unwanted sexual contact.

[31] Those cited by at least 20 percent of the 87 servicemembers.

[32] Adultery in the military is punishable under Article 134, UCMJ. Underage drinking is punishable under Article 134 or Article 92, UCMJ.

[33] GAO-08-924.

[34] Response Systems to Adult Sexual Assault Crimes Panel, Report of the Response Systems to Adult Sexual Assault Crimes Panel (June 2014). The Response Systems Panel is a federal advisory committee established by the Secretary of Defense in response to section 576 of

the National Defense Authorization Act for Fiscal Year 2013 (Pub. L. No. 112-239) to conduct an independent review and assessment of the systems used to investigate, prosecute, and adjudicate crimes involving adult sexual assault and related offenses under article 120 of the Uniform Code of Military Justice.

[35] GAO-05-927. To identify these practices, we reviewed relevant literature including previous GAO reports, spoke with experts in using performance information, and held group discussions with federal program managers. We also interviewed individuals within five federal agencies and reviewed documentation to illustrate how program managers have used performance information to make decisions. We identified uses for performance information including identifying problems and taking action, developing strategy and allocating resources, recognizing and rewarding performance, and identifying and sharing effective approaches. See GAO-05-927 for additional details on our scope and methodology for identifying these practices.

[36] DOD has used the Workplace and Gender Relations Survey to estimate the past-year prevalence of unwanted sexual contact among active-duty service members. The Defense Manpower and Data Center administered the survey on a regular basis from 1995 through 2012. According to DOD's November 2014 Report to the President of the United States on Sexual Assault Prevention and Response, the leadership of the Senate Armed Services Committee requested that the 2014 survey be conducted by a non-DOD entity, and the department contracted with the RAND Corporation to conduct the survey. RAND officials told us that they expect future surveys to be again conducted by the Defense Manpower and Data Center.

[37] "Reported incidents of sexual assault" refers to reports filed with DOD by individuals stating that they were sexually assaulted, whereas "prevalence" refers to the estimated incidence of either unwanted sexual contact, or, beginning in 2014, of sexual assault, whether reported or not. DOD—and in 2014, RAND on behalf of DOD—calculates prevalence estimates for the active-duty servicemember population based responses from surveys of active-duty servicemembers.

[38] GAO-08-924.

-10-215.

[40] Using results of the 2014 Military Workplace Study that the RAND Corporation conducted for DOD, we estimated that between 8 and 13 percent of active-duty male servicemembers and 39 to 44 percent of active-duty female servicemembers reported their sexual assaults.

[41] DOD, DOD-Wide Sexual Assault Prevention and Response (SAPR) Strategic Plan (2010-2015) (Aug. 1, 2009); and Sexual Assault Prevention and Response Strategic Plan (Apr. 30, 2013).

[42] See Secretary of Defense Memorandum, Sexual Assault Prevention and Response (May 1, 2014).

[43] See Pub. L. No. 108-375, §577 (2004).

[44] DOD Directive 6495.01. DOD first issued this directive in October 2005. The directive was reissued on January 23, 2012, and continues to specify the various types of care available to servicemembers in the aftermath of a sexual assault.

[45] U.S. Department of Justice, Office on Violence Against Women, A National Protocol for Sexual Assault Medical Forensic Examinations, Adults/Adolescents (April 2013).

[46] DODI 6495.02. DOD first issued this instruction in June 2006. The directive was reissued on March 28, 2013, and continues to specifically include guidance on providing medical care to sexual assault victims.

[47] Safe Helpline is owned by DOD and operated through a contractual agreement with the nonprofit Rape, Abuse, and Incest National Network (RAINN).

[48] At each of our four visits to military installations, military health-care providers said that they had long treated sexual assault victims as emergency cases, even prior to the DOD policy.

[49] GAO-13-182.

[50] This facility operates one of the few residential programs that specifically treats male veterans with post-traumatic stress disorder as a result of military sexual trauma.

[51] We conducted a literature review of academic and research articles published from January 2008 through September 2014 that addressed male victims' responses to sexual assault in order to identify and summarize existing findings and research on gender differences in sexual assault responses as well as male-victim needs. We selected these dates to match the period of data we reviewed during this review. Using a variety of academic databases, we searched using terms related to males, sexual assault victims, and sexual assault. We excluded those articles that discussed only female sexual assault victims or child abuse victims, or any that did not discuss male sexual assault victims or victim responses and needs following sexual assault.

[52] Karen G. Weiss, "Male Sexual Victimization: Examining Men's Experiences of Rape and Sexual Assault," Men and Masculinities, vol. 12, no. 3 (April 2010), 275–98.

[53] Barry Wall, MD, "Commentary: Causes and Consequences of Male Adult Sexual Assault," Journal of the American Academy of Psychiatry Law, vol. 39 (2011), 206–8.

[54] Tara E. Galovski et al., "Sex differences in recovery from PTSD in male and female interpersonal assault survivors," Behaviour Research and Therapy, vol. 51 (2013), 247–255.

[55] Iain A. McLean, PhD, "The male victim of sexual assault," Best Practice & Research Clinical Obstetrics and Gynaecology, vol. 27 (2013), 39–45.

[56] C. M. Bullock and M. Beckson, "Male Victims of Sexual Assault: Phenomenology, Psychology, Physiology," Journal of the American Academy of Psychiatry Law, vol. 39 (2011), 197–205.

[57] Military sexual trauma is a term based in part on federal law used by the VA and is defined as "psychological trauma, which in the judgment of a mental health professional employed by the department, resulted from a physical assault of a sexual nature, battery of a sexual nature, or sexual harassment ("repeated, unsolicited verbal or physical contact of a sexual nature which is threatening in character") that occurred while the veteran was serving on active duty or active duty for training or inactive duty training." See 38 U.S.C § 1720D.

[58] Carol O'Brien et al., "Difficulty identifying feelings predicts persistence of trauma symptoms in a sample of veterans who experienced military sexual trauma," Journal of Nervous and Mental Disease, vol. 196 (2008), 252–255.

[59] Galovski et al., "Sex differences in recovery from PTSD in male and female interpersonal assault survivors."

[60] GAO-13-182.

[61] GAO/GGD-00-204. To identify these leading practices, we conducted case studies of how some agencies have already used evaluation studies and methods in their performance reports. Based on the cases we reviewed, we identified that evaluations were generally used to develop or improve upon agencies' measures of program performance or to better understand performance and how it might be improved. See GAO/GGD-00-204 for additional details on our scope and methodology for identifying these practices.

[62] Office of the Army Surgeon General, The Concerns of Women Currently Serving in the Afghanistan Theater of Operations (2011).

[63] Anne G. Sadler, Combat, Sexual Assault, and Post-Traumatic Stress in OIF/OEF Military Women (Iowa City VA Research Foundation, January 2013). As a contracted study, the views are attributed to the author.

[64] Cynthia LeardMann et al., "Combat Deployment Is Associated with Sexual Harassment or Sexual Assault in a Large, Female Military Cohort," Women's Health Issues (May 2013). As a contracted study, the views are attributed to the author.

[65] Assistant Secretary of Defense for Health Affairs, Report to Congress, Review of Gender- and Ethnic Group-Specific Mental Health Services and Treatment for Members of the Armed Forces (August 2008).

[66] Department of Defense, Sexual Assault Prevention Strategy: Creating a National Benchmark Program (Sept. 30, 2008).

[67] GAO, Results-Oriented Government: Practices That Can Help Enhance and Sustain Collaboration among Federal Agencies, GAO-06-15 (Washington, D.C.: Oct. 21, 2005). To identify these leading practices, we reviewed relevant literature, including our prior reports, and interviewed experts in the area of collaboration. See GAO-06-15 for additional details on our scope and methodology for identifying these practices.

[68] GAO, Standards for Internal Control in the Federal Government, GAO/AIMD-00-21.3.1 (Washington, D.C.: November 1999).

[69] See Department of Defense, 2014-2016 Sexual Assault Prevention Strategy (Apr. 30, 2014).

[70] We reviewed the following GAO reports related to creating results-oriented cultures and effecting organization change: GAO-04-546G. For that report, we sought the input of outside experts, including from the Office of Personnel Management, in outlining a framework that summarizes the attributes of an effective training program. GAO-03-669. For that report, we convened a forum to identify useful practices and lessons learned from major private- and public-sector organizational mergers, acquisitions, and transformations. GAO-03-293SP. For that report, we convened a forum to identify useful practices from major private- and public-sector organizational mergers, acquisitions, and transformations. GAO/NSIAD-92-105. For that report, we obtained the views of private-sector experts on techniques used to change or perpetuate an organizational culture.

[71] Defense Task Force on Sexual Assault in the Military Services, Report of the Defense Task Force on Sexual Assault in the Military Services (Dec. 1, 2009).

[72] DOD, 2014-2016 Sexual Assault Prevention Strategy.

[73] The report did not make any recommendations directed at this concern.

[74] See, for example, GAO, Gender Issues: Information on DOD's Assignment Policy and Direct Ground Combat Definition, GAO/NSIAD-99-7 (Washington, D.C.: Oct. 19, 1998); Women in the Military: Deployment in the Persian Gulf War, GAO/NSIAD-93-93 (Washington, D.C.: July 13, 1993); and Women in the Military: More Military Jobs Can Be Opened Under Current Statuses, GAO/NSIAD-88-222 (Washington, D.C.: Sept. 7, 1988). In addition, Congress mandated GAO to review the progress military services are making in opening closed positions and occupations to women and in developing gender-neutral occupational standards, and to review military recruiting efforts to increase accessions of women into the officer corps. Results of this work are expected in 2015.

[75] This policy, commonly known as "Don't Ask, Don't Tell," based on 10 U.S.C. §654, was repealed on September 20, 2011.

[76] GAO-03-669.

[77] GAO/NSIAD-92-105.

[78] GAO-03-669.

[79] See, for example, GAO-03-669 and GAO/NSIAD-92-105.

[80] DOD, The Department of Defense Sexual Assault Prevention Strategy: Creating a National Benchmark Program.

[81] DOD, Department of Defense Annual Report on Sexual Assault in the Military: Fiscal Year 2013.

[82] The Senate Armed Services Committee has mandated GAO to review the April 2014 prevention strategy, and the results of this work are expected to be issued in 2015. See S. Rep. No. 113-176 at 115 (2014).

[83] GAO-03-669.

[84] GAO/NSIAD-92-105.

[85] The SAPRO website did not include the posters for 2010 or 2013.

[86] GAO-04-546G.

[87] DOD Instruction 6495.02.

[88] DOD Instruction 6495.02.

[89] For further information on our survey and scenarios, see app. II.

End Notes for Appendix I

[1] Because we did not select locations using a statistically representative sampling method, the comments provided during our interviews with installation officials are nongeneralizable and therefore cannot be projected across DOD, a service, or any single installation we visited. While the information obtained was not generalizable, it provided perspectives from installation officials that may have come into contact with male sexual assault victims.

[2] GAO, Managing for Results: Enhancing Agency Use of Performance Information for Management Decision Making, GAO-05-927 (Washington, D.C.: Sept. 9, 2005). To develop these leading practices, we reviewed relevant literature including previous GAO reports, spoke with experts in using performance information, and held group discussions with federal program managers. We also interviewed individuals within five federal agencies and reviewed documentation to illustrate how program managers have used performance information to make decisions. We identified uses for performance information including identifying problems and taking action, developing strategy and allocating resources, recognizing and rewarding performance, and identifying and sharing effective approaches. See GAO-05-927 for additional details on the development of these practices.

[3] The interviewer-administered surveys were one-on-one interviews that were administered in-person by an interviewer reading aloud the questions and, when applicable, available responses, from the survey. The interviews were conducted from May 2014 through August 2014.

[4] As of December 2014, we interviewed 12 male victims who voluntarily contacted us to discuss being sexually assaulted while serving in the U.S. military. We announced GAO's interest in anonymously interviewing male servicemembers who experienced sexual assault and provided a toll-free telephone number and email address for volunteers to contact us. Officials in DOD's Sexual Assault Prevention and Response Office (SAPRO), the department's lead office for sexual assault prevention and response, volunteered to post our announcement on the DOD Safe Helpline website, and we also disseminated the announcement through program and installation officials, advocacy groups, and subject-matter experts. Because we did not select participants using a statistically representative

sampling method, the perspectives obtained are nongeneralizable and therefore cannot be projected across DOD or an individual branch of service. While the information obtained was not generalizable, it provided perspectives from male sexual assault victims who were willing to discuss how serving in the military may have affected their decision to report that they were sexually assaulted as well as their experience seeking assistance and care.

[5] We did not use data prior to fiscal year 2008 because DOD did not report on the victim gender of all unrestricted sexual assault reports involving servicemember victims until fiscal year 2008. Fiscal year 2014 was the most recent complete year of data available.

[6] DOD reports these estimates as a single figure with a range of error. We calculated the possible ranges of DOD's estimates and used these figures in order to reflect the uncertainty surrounding the estimates.

[7] DOD has used the Workplace and Gender Relations Survey of Active Duty Members (WGRA) to estimate the past-year prevalence of unwanted sexual contact among active duty service members. WGRA surveys for fiscal years 2010 and 2012 were conducted by the Defense Manpower Data Center and the 2014 survey was conducted by the RAND Corporation. RAND administered a survey measuring unwanted sexual contact in fiscal year 2014 in order to compare to previous WGRA surveys that measured unwanted sexual contact. In addition, in an effort to address some of the criticisms made of the 2012 WGRA and prior versions of that survey, and to make the focus of the survey more clearly on crimes under the U.S. military legal code—the Uniform Code of Military Justice—the RAND Corporation administered another survey that measured the prevalence of sexual assault in fiscal year 2014. "Reported incidents of sexual assault" refers to known occurrences of such crimes whereas "prevalence" refers to the estimated incidence of sexual assault, whether reported or not, that DOD calculates based on experiences of unwanted sexual contact that are anonymously reported by servicemembers on the department's Workplace and Gender Relations Survey.

[8] We met with outside experts and advocacy groups with experience working with male victims that were identified through our prior work in the area of sexual assault in the military, in our literature review, and by DOD officials. During our installation visits, we met with civilian health-care providers that were located near the installations we visited. The views they expressed in our meetings are not generalizable to any group of experts or advocates.

[9] GAO, Program Evaluation: Studies Helped Agencies Measure or Explain Program Performance, GAO/GGD-00-204 (Washington, D.C.: Sept. 29, 2000). To develop these leading practices, we conducted case studies of how some agencies have already used evaluation studies and methods in their performance reports. Based on the cases we reviewed, we identified that evaluations were generally used to develop or improve upon agencies' measures of program performance or to better understand performance and how it might be improved. See GAO/GGD-00-204 for additional details on the scope and methodology used for identifying these practices.

[10] We selected this timeframe to align with the years of data we reviewed and analyzed for this report.

[11] Posters for 2010 and 2013 were not available on the website at the time of our review.

[12] We reviewed the following GAO reports related to creating results-oriented cultures and effecting organization change: GAO, Human Capital: A Guide for Assessing Strategic Training and Development Efforts in the Federal Government, GAO-04-546G (Washington, D.C.: Mar. 1, 2004). For that report, we sought the input of outside experts, including from the Office of Personnel Management, in outlining a framework that summarizes the attributes of an effective training program. GAO, Results-Oriented

Cultures: Implementation Steps to Assist Mergers and Organizational Transformations, GAO-03-669 (Washington, D.C.: July 2, 2003). For that report, we convened a forum to identify useful practices and lessons learned from major private- and public-sector organizational mergers, acquisitions, and transformations. GAO, Mergers and Transformation: Lessons Learned for a Department of Homeland Security and Other Federal Agencies, GAO-03-293SP (Washington, D.C.: Nov. 14, 2002). For that report, we convened a forum to identify useful practices from major private- and public-sector organizational mergers, acquisitions, and transformations. GAO, Organizational Culture: Techniques Companies Use to Perpetuate or Change Beliefs or Values, GAO/NSIAD-92-105 (Washington, D.C.: Feb. 27, 1992). For that report, we obtained the views of private sector experts on techniques used to change or perpetuate an organizational culture.

End Note for Appendix II

[1] Participants were categorized according to the following ranks: junior enlisted (encompassing the ranks of E1–E4); senior enlisted (encompassing the ranks of E5–E7); junior officers (encompassing the ranks of O1–O3); and senior officers (encompassing the ranks of O4–O5).

In: Sexual Assaults of Male Military Personnel ISBN: 978-1-63483-564-0
Editor: Henrietta Moore

Chapter 2

RESPONSE TO THE U.S. GOVERNMENT ACCOUNTABILITY OFFICE'S REPORT ON MALE VICTIMS*

Department of Defense

INTRODUCTION

In March 2015, the U.S. Government Accountability Office (GAO) released a report titled "Military Personnel: Actions Needed to Address Sexual Assaults of Male Servicemembers."[1] The report presents six recommendations for improving the Department of Defense's (DoD) sexual assault prevention and response (SAPR) services with respect to male Service members. The following document outlines GAO's recommendations and responds to each with the progress DoD has already made in addressing GAO's concerns. This document also discusses plans for future DoD action to address male sexual assault victimization.

---

* This is an edited, reformatted and augmented version of material that appeared as Appendix C to the Department of Defense Annual Report on Sexual Assault in the Military, Fiscal Year 2014; issued to Congress May 1, 2015.

GAO RECOMMENDATION 1: DATA-DRIVEN DECISION MAKING

"To help DOD's sexual assault prevention and response program realize the full benefit of the data it collects on sexual assault incidents, we recommend that the Secretary of Defense direct the Under Secretary of Defense for Personnel and Readiness, in collaboration with the Secretaries of the military services, to develop a plan for data-driven decision making to prioritize program efforts."

DoD integrates responsive, comprehensive, and rigorous systems of measurement and analysis into every aspect of the SAPR program. Over the past few years, DoD has built a foundation of data sources to address male victimization. In the forthcoming years, we will use these information streams to better shape policy and programs for male victims. The following sections summarize current data sources that inform SAPR policy and programs.

DEFENSE SEXUAL ASSAULT INCIDENT DATABASE

In accordance with the fiscal year (FY) 2009 National Defense Authorization Act (NDAA), DoD created the Defense Sexual Assault Incident Database (DSAID), a secure internet database designed for reporting and case management of sexual assaults committed by or against Service members. Using DSAID, DoD can analyze sexual assault incident data with greater depth and precision than ever before. For instance, DSAID has given DoD greater visibility over the type of sexual assault reports made by male and female victims (Table 1).

Table 1. Sexual Assault Reporting by Victim Gender and Status

	Male	*Female*	*Gender Data Not Available*	*Total*
All Reports	1208	4852	71	6131
Service Member Victims	1180	4104	0	5284
Incidents Occurring Prior to Service	98	418	0	516
Non-Service Member Victims	14	731	0	745
Data on Victim Service Status Unavailable	14	17	71	102

	Male	*Female*	*Gender Data Not Available*	*Total*
Unrestricted Reports	965	3628	67	4660
Service Member Victims	937	2914	0	3851
Incidents Occurring Prior to Service	41	94	0	135
Non-Service Member Victims	14	698	0	712
Data on Victim Service Status Unavailable	14	16	67	97
Reports Remaining Restricted	243	1224	4	1471
Service Member Victims	243	1190	0	1433
Incidents Occurring Prior to Service	57	324	0	381
Non-Service Member Victims	0	33	0	33
Data on Victim Service Status Unavailable	0	1	4	5
Restricted Reports Converted to Unrestricted (Included in Unrestricted Total)	45	288	36	369
Service Member Victims	45	279	0	324
Non-Service Member Victims	0	9	0	9
Data on Victim Service Status Unavailable	0	0	36	36

DoD is exploring analytic options to better understand and summarize the vast amount of information stored in DSAID. Analyses focused on gender differences can inform DoD about the unique needs of male and female victims who report their sexual assault. These analyses can investigate whether significant demographic differences exist between male and female victims and their alleged perpetrators, whether the characteristics of sexual assault incidents vary by victim gender, and whether SAPR response efforts (e.g., referrals and services offered) differ by victim gender. Furthermore, these analyses allow DoD to compare survey data on sexual assault prevalence estimates to reporting statistics.

It is important to note that DSAID only tracks the subset of victims who made a report of sexual assault. The data on male victims may be particularly sparse because male Service members are less likely to report sexual assault than female Service members. As such, DoD relies on scientific population surveys to determine sexual assault prevalence and assess the experience of sexual assault victims.

WORKPLACE AND GENDER RELATIONS SURVEY/RAND MILITARY WORKPLACE STUDY

From Calendar Year (CY) 2006 to FY 2012, the Defense Manpower Data Center (DMDC) assessed the prevalence of unwanted sexual contact (USC) using the *Workplace and Gender Relations Survey of Active Duty Members* (*WGRA*). USC is the DMDC survey term for the range of sexual crimes between adults, prohibited by military law, ranging from abusive sexual contact to rape. In its earliest iterations, some *WGRA* estimates were unreportable due to small sample sizes. More recently, DMDC sampled a greater proportion of Service members to allow for detailed analyses on small subsamples of interest, such as men who indicated they had experienced USC.

DoD contracted the RAND Corporation (RAND) to administer the *RAND Military Workplace Study* (*RMWS*) to determine the prevalence of sexual assault in FY 2014. At the request of DoD, RAND sampled the entire population of active duty women and 25% of active duty men. The unprecedentedly large number of male Service member respondents gave RAND the ability to perform more detailed and reliable demographic analyses compared to past surveys. When describing the new RAND prevalence survey below, we refer to sexual assault, rather than USC, because the RAND survey measure was designed to more closely align with the language used to describe sexual assault crimes under the Uniform Code of Military Justice (UCMJ).

The FY 2014 *RMWS* identified important differences between the sexual assault experiences of male and female Service members. Overall, men are more likely than women to indicate that the sexual assault was perpetrated by multiple offenders and to describe the incident as "hazing." Male sexual assault victims also indicated that the sexual assault occurred in the workplace and without the use of alcohol. Some male victims who experience such hazing/bullying incidents may not consider making a report because they may not identify the incident as a sexual assault. In addition, men are more likely than women to experience violent or abusive sexual assaults when that assault is penetrative.

Lastly, among both male and female victims, an experience of past-year sexual assault was highly correlated with an experience of past-year sexual harassment; however, the relationship between sexual assault and sexual harassment was stronger for male victims. For more details about gender differences in sexual assault experiences, see RAND's report in Annex 1.

SERVICE ACADEMY GENDER RELATIONS SURVEY

DoD assesses the prevalence of USC at the Military Service Academies (MSAs) through the *Service Academy Gender Relations Survey* (*SAGR*), administered by DMDC. For the first time in 2014, *SAGR* sampled the entire population of male and female cadets/midshipmen, generating a much higher number of male respondents than past surveys. The large sample of male *SAGR* respondents enabled DMDC to conduct more thorough and complete analyses of the experiences of male victims than in past survey iterations. Across the MSA population, estimated past-year prevalence of USC was down significantly for both male and female cadets/midshipmen.

Compared to female cadets/midshipmen victims, a higher percentage of male cadets/midshipmen victims indicated that their sexual assault was a hazing incident and/or that it involved some form of "horseplay," locker room behavior, or other similar behaviors. Furthermore, compared to female cadets/midshipmen victims, fewer male cadets/midshipmen victims at each Academy indicated that they or their alleged offender(s) had been drinking alcohol at the time of the incident that had the greatest impact on them. Finally, similar to the *RMWS*, a strong relationship between experiences of sexual harassment/sexist behavior and sexual assault was observed in the *2014 SAGR*. For more details about the *2014 SAGR*, see DMDC's "2014 Service Academy Gender Relations Survey Report."[2]

SURVIVOR EXPERIENCE SURVEY AND MILITARY JUSTICE EXPERIENCE SURVEY

In 2014, DoD administered the *Survivor Experience Survey* (*SES*) to examine the experiences of Service members who made a Restricted or Unrestricted Report of sexual assault. The *SES* is the first survey of its kind, providing DoD with greater visibility over male and female sexual assault survivors' experiences with DoD's response process on a continual basis.[3] Furthermore, DoD developed the *Military Justice Experience Survey* (*MJES*) to learn about survivors' experiences with the justice system. Participant recruitment for the *MJES* will begin in Spring or Summer of 2015 and will proceed on a continual, long-term basis.

Defense Equal Opportunity Management Institute Organizational Climate Survey

The Defense Equal Opportunity Management Institute Organizational Climate Survey (DEOCS) provides commanders with a unique opportunity to receive anonymous feedback from their unit on a wide variety of topics related to equal opportunity and organizational effectiveness, including the unit's perceptions of command support of the SAPR program. Although between 100,000 and 200,000 personnel take the DEOCS each month, respondents may not be completely representative of the force as a whole. Nonetheless, the DEOCS is a useful tool, particularly for individual unit commanders, to assess SAPR program progress.

Analyses of DEOCS data are presented by gender, which often demonstrate small but important differences between men and women's perceptions of command climate. Overall, Service members perceive a favorable command climate with respect to SAPR; however, male Service members tend to have a more positive view than their female counterparts. To a greater extent than female Service members, male Service members indicated that their chain of command promoted a climate based on "respect and trust" free of sexist behaviors, believed that retaliation against victims of sexual assault was unlikely in their unit, and thought that their command supported sexual assault prevention and response.

Health Related Behaviors Survey of Active Duty Military Personnel

The *Health Related Behaviors Survey of Active Duty Military Personnel* (*HRB*) examines health issues relevant to the wellbeing and readiness of the Services. Recent analyses of the 2011 survey, sponsored by DoD's Sexual Assault Prevention and Response Office (SAPRO), the Defense Suicide Prevention Office, and the United States Coast Guard, focused on sexual assault victimization and health behavior in the Services. According to the *HRB*, both male and female Service members who experienced sexual assault, both before and after joining the military, were more likely to report suicidal ideation, suicide attempts, and post-traumatic stress than those with no history of sexual assault. Furthermore, those with a history of sexual assault victimization were more likely to indicate that they needed and/or received mental health services than those with no history of sexual assault. However, of those victims who received mental health services, a significant minority (33% among men and 27% among women) perceived that seeking mental health services negatively affected their military careers.[4]

An experience of sexual assault had important implications for the career attitudes of sexual assault victims, particularly among men. Men who experienced sexual assault after joining the military exhibited lower career commitment (as measured by self-reported intent to remain in the military) compared to men who were not assaulted. The difference in career commitment between women who had been sexually assaulted and those who had not been assaulted was not statistically significant.

SECTION SUMMARY

The breadth of data sources summarized above demonstrates DoD's strong commitment to data-driven decision making. With this solid foundation, DoD's analytic capabilities will continue to grow and become more robust as annual data are collected and trend analyses are conducted.

GAO RECOMMENDATIONS 2 AND 3: GENDER-SPECIFIC TREATMENTS FOR SEXUAL ASSAULT VICTIMS

> "To help ensure that all of DOD's medical and mental health providers are generally aware of any gender-specific needs of sexual assault victims, and that victims are provided the care that most effectively meets those needs, we are recommending that the Assistant Secretary of Defense for Health Affairs, in collaboration with the services' Surgeons General,
>
> - Systematically evaluate the extent to which differences exist in the medical and mental health care needs of male and female sexual assault victims, and the care regimen, if any, that will best meet those needs; and
> - Develop and issue guidance for the department's medical and mental health providers—and other personnel, as appropriate—based on the results of this evaluation that delineates these gender-

specific distinctions and the care regimen that is recommended to most effectively meet those needs."

DoD is committed to fully understanding the needs of both male and female victims to further improve its response services and treatment programs. A review of the research literature, DoD-sponsored research, and extant treatment approaches within the Veterans Administration provides important insights about the different needs of male and female victims. DoD will continue to explore different approaches to best treat sexual assault victims and will issue guidance to expand its current approach.

REVIEW OF RESEARCH ON TREATMENT APPROACHES FOR MALE VICTIMS

Although men and women experience many of the same psychological difficulties due to sexual assault victimization, they also face distinct challenges.[5] Male victims of sexual assault may have difficulty reconciling their masculine identity—normatively associated with strength and control—with the experience of being a victim.[6,7] Furthermore, male victims may struggle with their sexual identity, and treatment needs may vary depending on victims' sexual orientation and the gender of their perpetrators.[8] As summarized in the prior section, DoD-sponsored research (*RMWS* and *SAGR*) suggests that the nature of sexual assault experienced by men versus women varies in important ways. Overall, men are more likely than women to experience sexual assault allegedly perpetrated by multiple offenders and described as "hazing."

Widely endorsed myths suggesting that men cannot be raped or should be able to defend themselves against rape likely deter male victims from reporting their sexual assault.[9,10] Male victims may fear that they will face disbelief, blame, and scorn if they choose to report.[11] Additionally, male victims who experience sexual assault during incidents of hazing or bullying may not consider reporting the experience because of the misperception that the incident is not a "sexual" assault. When men do seek medical attention after a sexual assault, they often seek assistance for secondary injuries without revealing the sexual assault that led to those injuries.[12] Research on the civilian population suggests that societally-endorsed myths about rape even persist among service providers, including counselors, crisis workers, medical personnel and law enforcement officials.[13,14,15]

Collectively, the research described above suggests the need for improved outreach to male victims and enhanced training for service providers.[16] Expanded training for professionals who work with sexual assault victims can increase awareness and dispel widely endorsed myths about male rape. For example, medical personnel may require specific education on how to examine male victims and collect evidence.[17] Given that male victims may seek medical attention for injuries resulting from a sexual assault without referencing the sexual assault, more subtle ways to ask about and detect medical conditions associated with sexual assault victimization could be incorporated into general medical visits.

Additionally, treatment approaches for male victims may need to address gender and sexual identity issues and externalizing behaviors (e.g., alcohol and drug abuse, angry outbursts, self-harm, etc.) that male victims may exhibit more frequently than female victims.[18, 19] Finally, tailoring treatments may better address the needs of individuals regardless of gender. For example, the circumstances of the assault, the gender of the alleged perpetrator, and the sexual orientation of the victim may be important factors to consider when developing treatment approaches for both male and female victims.[20]

DEPARTMENT OF VETERANS AFFAIRS' APPROACH TO MALE VICTIMS

In addition to considering empirical research on treating sexual assault, DoD also examines existing treatment programs for sexual assault victims to inform its policies. The Department of Veterans Affairs has a well-known program to treat male and female victims of sexual assault. Along with residential facilities that specialize in sexual assault and male victim care[21], practitioners at outpatient Veterans Affairs centers across the country treat male victims where they reside. Specialists at the Department of Veterans Affairs emphasize that there is no "one size fits all" treatment approach to treating sexual assault victims. Since each victim has specific needs, the tailoring of treatment approaches should primarily depend on the individual's symptoms and needs. The Department of Veterans Affairs trains providers to recognize the unique experiences of male sexual assault victims, while at the same time appreciating the wide variability in responses to sexual assault.[22]

In recent years, the Department of Veterans Affairs has found it beneficial to offer mixed-gender group therapy in residential facilities while also providing the time and space for same-gender process groups. This approach, however, may not suit the needs of all victims and requires highly skilled providers to manage and deliver patient care in this setting. Some victims may prefer a mixed-gender approach, while others may want to meet with men only or women only. Still others may prefer to solely address the *symptoms* of their sexual assault, and may join groups that focus on general trauma, Posttraumatic Stress Disorder (PTSD), or depression.

SECTION SUMMARY

Support services for and research on male victims of sexual assault has yet to reach the level of services for and research on female victims. As such, DoD is considering various approaches to close this gap in knowledge and provide specific guidance on treating male victims.

GAO RECOMMENDATIONS 4, 5 AND 6: ADDRESS MALE SEXUAL ASSAULT VICTIMIZATION IN SAPR TRAINING, COMMUNICATION AND STRATEGY

> "To address challenges faced by male servicemembers as DOD continues to seek to transform its culture to address sexual assault, we are recommending that the Secretary of Defense direct the Under Secretary of Defense for Personnel and Readiness, in collaboration with the Secretaries of the military services, to:
>
> - Develop clear goals with associated metrics to drive the changes needed to address sexual assaults of males and articulate these goals, for example in the department's next sexual assault prevention strategy;
> - Include information about the sexual victimization of males in communications to servicemembers that are used to raise awareness of sexual assault and the department's efforts to prevent and respond to it; and
> - Revise sexual assault prevention and response training to more comprehensively and directly address the incidence of male servicemembers being sexually assaulted and how certain behavior and activities—like hazing—can lead to a sexual assault."

As discussed in the previous sections, DoD sponsors a variety of research initiatives to understand gender differences in sexual victimization. These research initiatives will inform prevention strategy and help DoD convey a more realistic picture of male sexual assault victimization in training programs and communications to Service members. Additionally, the Department directed several initiatives to increase outreach to male victims and to evaluate prevention programming.

DEPARTMENT RESEARCH EFFORTS

DoD has a solid foundation of data sources to inform policy, training, and communication on male victims. The *SES* and the *MJES*, which are administered on a rolling basis, will provide information on the effectiveness of DoD's response process for male and female victims.

Both the *RMWS* and *SAGR* provide important insights about the different experiences of male and female sexual assault victims. Compared to female victims, male victims are more likely to associate their assault with abuse and humiliation, often in connection with hazing incidents. Furthermore, sexual victimization of male Service members is less likely to involve alcohol and more likely to occur in the workplace, compared to sexual victimization of female Service members. In addition, male Service members are more likely than female Service members to experience violent or abusive sexual assaults when that assault is penetrative. For male and female victims alike, those who experience sexual harassment are more likely to experience sexual assault than those with no history of sexual harassment. This correlation is particularly strong for male victims of sexual assault.

One of the primary conclusions coming from the *RMWS* is that many men may perceive and experience sexual assault differently than most women. Men's experiences with sexual assault were not fully understood until the *RMWS* asked about them using specific language and behaviors derived from military law. The results of the *RMWS* indicated that although many men experienced oral and anal penetration, they do not necessarily perceive these acts as "sexual." Instead, many of these acts are consistent with hazing and meant to humiliate the victim rather than to stimulate the alleged offender. Men in these circumstances may see little need for help from a "sexual assault" program or a "victim advocate," because they may perceive these behaviors as non-sexual misconduct. This understanding may require DoD to examine its sexual assault prevention and response system to determine if corresponding program and policy modifications lead to greater reporting by men.

The results of Department-sponsored survey efforts suggest several avenues for improvement of SAPR strategies. DoD can expand awareness of male sexual assault victimization by communicating that hazing and bullying experiences can constitute a sexual assault crime under the UCMJ. Although male Service members account for the majority of the survey-estimated victims of sexual assault, a greater proportion of female victims report their assault (about 43% of women versus about 10% of men in FY 2014). By broadening Service members' understanding of sexual assault and emphasizing that sexual assaults do not necessarily center on sexual gratification of the alleged perpetrator(s), male Service members will be better equipped to recognize and report sexual assault crimes when they occur. Furthermore, greater awareness about male victimization among leadership and SAPR first responders may help to improve the response process for male victims who do report.

This new knowledge about gender differences in sexual assault experiences can inform prevention strategy and training. Hazing and bullying may be a key area of focus with respect to prevention. Additionally, given that sexual assault victimization is often associated with sexual harassment and gender discrimination, prevention efforts should center on eliminating a broad range of gender-based sexual maltreatment.

SECRETARY OF DEFENSE INITIATIVES

In May 2014, the Secretary of Defense at the time directed the Secretaries of the Military Departments to take steps to improve reporting and encourage male victims to seek assistance, to include a request that the Secretaries solicit male victim input in the development of these methods. The Services have since acted on this directive and in January 2015, each of the Services provided their implementation plans to DoD. DoD is currently consolidating the submitted plans for review by Secretary Carter. Overall, all four Services resolved to increase the extent to which their prevention, education, and victim outreach efforts include information about male victims of sexual assault.

In December 2014, the Secretaries of the Military Departments were directed to implement the Installation Prevention Project (IPP) to advance DoD's understanding of successful intervention policies. The IPP will track prevention programming across select installations. This effort will help to identify promising practices for sexual assault prevention and allow the DoD to evaluate its prevention efforts.[23]

Conclusion

DoD is committed to a SAPR program that addresses the needs of *all* victims of sexual assault. New DoD research this year revealed the commonalities, as well as the differences, between the experiences of male and female victims. As the GAO recommends, DoD will continue to use data to inform policy, provide treatments that address specific victim needs, and develop new and innovative strategies to prevent and communicate the full range of sexual assault experiences.

End Notes

[1] Available at: http://www.gao.gov/products/GAO-15-284

[2] Available at: http://sapr.mil/index.php/research

[3] Available at: http://sapr.mil/index.php/research

[4] While these follow-up analyses did not have sufficient information to determine how respondents' military careers were affected by seeking mental health services, sexual assault produces more trauma symptoms than many other events, even high combat exposure (Kang, et al., 2005). Role of Sexual Assault on Risk of Post-Traumatic Stress Disorder among Gulf War Veterans, Annals of Epidemiology, 15, 191-195).

[5] Peterson, Z. D., Voller, E. K., Polusny, M. A., & Murdoch, M. (2011). Prevalence and consequences of adult sexual assault of men: Review of empirical findings and state of the literature. Clinical Psychology Review, 31, 1-24.

[6] Davies, M. (2002). Male sexual assault victims: A selective review of the literature and implications for support services. Aggression and Violent Behavior, 7, 203-214.

[7] Ibid. 5.

[8] Ibid. 6.

[9] Turchik, J. A., & Edwards, K. M. (2012). Myths about male rape: A literature review. Psychology of Men & Masculinity, 13, 211-226.

[10] Morris, E. E., Smith, J. C., Farooqui, S. Y., & Surís, A. M. (2013). Unseen battles: The recognition, assessment, and treatment issues of men with military sexual trauma (MST). Trauma, Violence, & Abuse, 15, 94-101.

[11] Ibid. 6.

[12] Isley, P. J., & Gehrenbeck-Shim, D. (1997). Sexual assault of men in the community. Journal of Community Psychology, 25, 159-166.

[13] Anderson, I., & Quinn, A. (2009). Gender differences in medical students' attitudes towards male and female rape victims. Psychology, Health & Medicine, 14, 105-110.

[14] Donnelly, D. A., & Kenyon, S. (1996). "Honey, we don't do men": Gender stereotypes and the provision of services to sexually assaulted males. Journal of Interpersonal Violence, 11, 441-448.

[15] Dye, E., & Roth, S. (1990). Psychotherapists' knowledge about and attitudes toward sexual assault victim clients. Psychology of Women Quarterly, 14, 191-212.

[16] Ibid. 10, p. 6.

[17] Ibid. 6, p. 6.

[18] Cucciare, M. A., Ghaus, S., Weingardt, K. R., & Frayne, S. M. (2011). Sexual assault and substance use in male veterans receiving a brief alcohol intervention. Journal of Studies on Alcohol and Drugs, 72, 693-700.

[19] Elliott, D. M., Mok, D. S., & Briere, J. (2004). Adult sexual assault: Prevalence, symptomology, and sex differences in the general population. Journal of Traumatic Stress, 17, 203–211

[20] Ibid. 6, p. 6.

[21] Bay Pines Veterans Affairs Healthcare System, located in Bay Pines, Florida at the C.W. Young Veterans Affairs Medical Center is one such center.

[22] This information was provided by the National Center for PTSD, U.S. Department of Veterans Affairs.

[23] The Public Health Model uses four-steps to address problems like sexual violence. Step 3 involves developing and testing prevention strategies. This approach is known as "evidence-based program planning," and ensures that prevention strategies are rigorously evaluated to determine effectiveness. See Dahlberg LL, Krug EG. "Violence-a global public health problem," In: Krug E, Dahlberg LL, Mercy JA, Zwi AB, Lozano R, eds. World Report on Violence and Health. Geneva, Switzerland: World Health Organization; 2002:1-56.

INDEX

A

B

C

I

L

M

N

O

P

Q

R

S

T

U

V

W

Y